URSULA FERRIGNO'S

trattoria

A PASSION FOR ITALIAN FOOD

URSULA FERRIGNO

RUNNING PRESS
PHILADELPHIA • LONDON

© 2006 by Octopus Publishing Group Limited
Text © 2006 by Ursula Ferrigno
Photographs © 2006 by Octopus Publishing Group Limited
First published in the United States in 2006 by Running Press Book Publishers
All rights reserved under the Pan-American and International Copyright
Conventions
Printed in China

9   8   7   6   5   4   3   2   1
Digit on the right indicates the number of this printing

Library of Congress Control Number: 2005931655

ISBN-13: 978-0-7624-2724-6
ISBN-10: 0-7624-2724-8

This book may be ordered by mail from the publisher. Please include $2.50
for postage and handling.
But try your bookstore first!

Running Press Book Publishers
125 South Twenty-second Street
Philadelphia, Pennsylvania 19103-4399

Commissioning Editor: Rebecca Spry
Executive Art Editor: Yasia Williams
Design: Miranda Harvey
Editor: Susan Fleming
Home Economy Assistant: Fizz Collins
Proof-reading: Diona Gregory
Production: Sarah Rogers
Index: John Noble
U.S. Edition Editor: Diana von Glahn
Photographs by Francesca Yorke

Typeset in Egyptienne and Bradley Hand
Printed and bound by Toppan Printing Company in China

Visit us on the web!
www.runningpress.com

thanks to..

Richard Moore, my husband – a constant source of
inspiration and goodness, not just in the kitchen.

Mummy, with her ever-ready willingness to listen and
understand.

Susan Fleming, a huge talent and such a pro, who is
great fun to work with. Susan is vital to my books –
endless thanks!

Working with Rebecca Spry just gets better. Ideas
flow and she has an ability to grasp a situation and
turn everything around so that it is just right.

Miranda Harvey, whose inspiration, intelligence and
aesthetic is beyond compare.

Francesca Yorke is a major talent – determined,
gentle, kind and fun, with a huge vision in every
sense of the word.

Fizz Collins, for providing such a wonderful venue for
the photo shoot, and for her help with the cooking.

Yasia Williams, who art directed the food shoot with
constant enthusiasm and a great eye.

Sam Hanna's ability to interpret what was needed
with the manuscript for the book; her speed,
determination and professionalism all made life so
much more pleasurable, particularly in the run-up to
my wedding.

Sam, Francesca's assistant, for tolerating such a lot of
women's chat, for his readiness and willingness to
help, and for his constant interest.

At Limelight, Fiona and Linda, for organizing yet
another great book for me.

contents

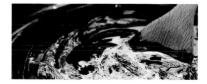

introduction

Italian cuisine is world-renowned for its use of superb seasonal ingredients and simple cooking methods. Apart from in the home, nowhere is this more apparent than in the cooking of Italy's local restaurants, the *trattorias*. In fact, the cooking in the best *trattorias* can be said to be as good as that in the home, for most are family-run. The majority of *trattorias* look comfortably domestic, with homey decorative touches – cloth tablecloths and napkins, personal pictures on the walls – and the food is far from sophisticated: seasonal, locally produced, simply cooked and always tasty.

Whether situated in the heart of a northern city or hidden away on a country road with an adjacent vineyard, the atmosphere of a *trattoria* is instantly familiar to all Italians and, increasingly, to visitors. The welcome is warm, the dining area is nothing fancy (often just a few tables under a canopy of vines in the country), and food is always the focus. Where the whole family might once have worked together, a kitchen might now be staffed by younger members, introducing a hint of modernity, but usually still under the watchful eye of the *nonna*. A *trattoria* today might offer a take-out service – usually foods *al forno* (straight from the oven) but cooked to the same impeccable standards – and some also offer rooms. One such *trattoria* I remember well: after lunch service was finished, the pasta was made, and drying strings of it festooned the tables and chairs in the dining room for the rest of the afternoon.

Trattoria cooking is home cooking at its best, and it can satisfy you and fill you up. Often the chefs or owners are determined to have you appreciate their skills or local dishes to the greatest extent. Francesca, the photographer for this book, tells of one place where, knowing there were at least five more courses to come, she left some of her pasta – much to her host's concern and dismay! Most *trattorias* will also be keen to have you taste their wines *de la casa*, often made nearby or by the family, and these can be delicious (although, sadly, not always).

The Slow Food movement, based in the north of Italy, has recently highlighted the unique position of *trattorias* in Italian life, awarding symbols for excellence. But whether given such accolades or not, most *trattorias* are the backbone of Italian eating: somewhere you can go for lunch every day and be assured of getting something different, something traditional, something reasonable in price, and something really well cooked. The recipes here – some from family-run *trattorias* we know or have found, some from friends' families and some my own – reflect that glorious creativity. In Italy, the *trattoria* remains the benchmark of good eating, and I hope these recipes will amply illustrate that truth.

soups, appetizers & antipasti

Soups are very popular in Italy, in family homes and in *trattorias*. The Piedmontese like to start a meal with soup, and their soups are delicious – based on chicken stock and thickened with rice from the Po or vegetables from the hills surrounding Turin.

tomato soup
minestrone di pomodori alla torinese

serves 4

1lb large, ripe tomatoes, skinned
  and coarsely chopped

1 garlic clove, peeled and finely chopped

a handful of fresh basil, torn

1 tbsp lemon juice

sea salt and freshly ground black pepper

¼ cup unsalted butter

3 tbsp all-purpose flour

3½ cups home-made chicken stock

1 tbsp tomato paste

1 Put the chopped tomatoes in a large pan with the garlic, basil, lemon juice and salt and pepper to taste. Cover the pan and bring to a boil, then lower the heat and simmer for 10 minutes. Allow to cool a little, then mix in a blender and set aside.

2 Melt the butter in a saucepan and stir in the flour. Let it cook for 2 minutes, then add the chicken stock, stirring all the time to keep the mixture smooth and lump-free. Stir in the tomatoes, cover and simmer for 10 minutes.

3 Put a little of the soup in a jug and dissolve the tomato paste in it. Add this to the pan and taste for seasoning. Simmer for 10 minutes, then serve.

little bread dumplings in broth
pasatelli

I first enjoyed this delicious soup at lunch before my friend Christiana got married. Her grandmother, Madellena Chapello, a great friend of mine and my father's, prepared it. This is a light, nutritious soup, usually served in the home or in *trattorias*.

serves 4

1½ cups fresh breadcrumbs

½ cup freshly grated Parmesan cheese, plus extra to serve

freshly grated nutmeg, to taste

sea salt and freshly ground black pepper

1 large egg, beaten

3½ cups vegetable stock

a good handful of fresh flat-leaf parsley, chopped

freshly torn basil, for garnish

1 To prepare the dumplings, on a large board mix together the breadcrumbs, Parmesan, nutmeg, and salt and pepper to taste. Make a well in the center, add the beaten egg and knead for about 3 minutes. Set aside.

2 Pour the stock into a large saucepan, add the parsley, then bring to a slow boil. Form the dumpling mixture into balls of about ½-inch in diameter. When the stock reaches the boiling point, cook the balls in batches, boiling each batch gently for 2 minutes. Remove from the heat and leave for at least a further 2 minutes.

3 Return the dumplings to the broth and serve with freshly grated Parmesan and freshly torn basil.

fresh zucchini soup with spaghetti

minestrone di zucchini con spaghetti

This is a pretty, colorful, light and tasty soup, which the Italians love to make when the zucchini season is in full swing, and they have more in the garden than they know what to do with. There are lots of varieties of zucchini in Italy: thick, thin, green, yellow, etc. My favorite is called *Roma*, which has a ridge on the skin. Whichever you buy, choose firm specimens, not too large, for maximum flavor.

serves 4

18 oz zucchini, washed
  and cut into ½-inch cubes
1 medium onion, peeled and
  chopped
2 tbsp olive oil
sea salt and freshly ground black
  pepper
6½ cups fresh vegetable broth
(see page 252)
1 x 28-oz can diced tomatoes
a handful of fresh basil leaves,
  torn
7 oz spaghetti, broken into
  1½-inch lengths
freshly grated Parmesan cheese

1 Put the zucchini, onion, olive oil and a little salt and pepper into a large saucepan, cover with the broth, and slowly bring to a boil. Reduce the heat to a simmer, and cook for 5 minutes.

2 Add the canned tomatoes and the basil, gently combine the ingredients, and slowly bring to a boil.

3 Add the spaghetti pieces, stir and cook over medium to high heat until the pasta is cooked – about 5 minutes. Stir once in a while. Check for seasoning.

4 Serve hot and pass around the Parmesan for people to sprinkle over their servings.

This recipe comes from Ester Gaffarelli at *Agriturismo la Luna e il Falò* in the Piedmontese village of Canelli. You may use pumpkin or butternut squash, but I love pumpkin. In Italy we store pumpkins in a cold place, covered with straw – they can last up to six months this way.

pumpkin soup
zuppa di zucca

serves 4

⅓ cup unsalted butter

1lb 7 oz butternut squash or
   pumpkin, peeled and seeded

2 medium carrots, peeled and
   diced into ½-inch pieces

1 medium onion, peeled and diced
   into ½-inch pieces

1 large celery stalk, diced into
   ½-inch pieces

4¼ cups chicken broth
   (see page 253)

sea salt and freshly ground black
   pepper

4 oz Swiss cheese, cubed
   into ½-inch pieces

4 tbsp freshly grated Parmesan

1 Melt the butter in a pan, add the pumpkin, carrots, onion and celery, and cook over medium-to-high heat, stirring often, until the onion is lightly golden – about 7-8 minutes.

2 Add the broth and season with salt and pepper. Bring the mixture to a boil, reduce the heat, and simmer uncovered for 45 minutes.

3 Ladle the hot soup into four individual bowls. Spoon a little Swiss cheese and Parmesan over each. Let the soup rest for 5 minutes before serving. Sometimes you may like to add croutons (see pages 12-13).

This recipe is based on a dish from the *Ristorante Solferino* in Tuscany, and it uses what they call "*duchese*" olive oil. This is made from olives grown on their own land and pressed locally. It is named after a family member, and is of very high quality. Use the best extra virgin oil you can get.

chicken and roasted pepper soup
zuppa di pollo con peperoni arrosto

serves 6

12 red peppers

10 chicken thighs

sea salt and freshly ground
  black pepper

2 tbsp olive oil

1 onion, peeled and chopped

2 garlic cloves, peeled and crushed

6⅓ cups chicken broth
  (see page 253), warm

a handful of fresh basil leaves, torn

a handful of fresh mint leaves,
  roughly chopped

2 tsp fresh marjoram leaves

duchese oil or good-quality
  extra virgin olive oil

1 Preheat the oven to 400°F. Roast the peppers for 25 minutes, then leave to cool. Scrape out the seeds and slice the peppers thinly.

2 At the same time, cook the chicken thighs. Season them with salt and pepper and roast alongside the peppers for 20 minutes, or until cooked through. Cool. Discard the chicken skin and bones and shred the meat finely.

3 Heat the oil in a large saucepan, add the onion and sauté until golden. Add the strips of peppers and the garlic.

4 Add the broth to the peppers along with the chicken shreds and herbs. Adjust the seasoning and simmer the soup for 5 minutes. Ladle into warmed soup bowls and serve with some good oil on top.

fish soup with macaroni
zuppa di pesce con pasta

Every *trattoria* the length and breadth of the coastline of Italy will serve a fish soup like this – perfectly plain, pure and simple. My grandmother, who came from Venice, would serve us fish soups quite regularly, saying it was good for our brains!

serves 4

9 oz monkfish steaks

9 oz boneless cod steaks

9 oz sea bass fillets

a generous handful of fresh
  flat-leaf parsley, finely chopped

2 tbsp olive oil

1 medium onion, peeled and
  chopped

2 garlic cloves, peeled and
  chopped

1 x 14.50-oz can diced tomatoes

sea salt and freshly ground black
  pepper

7 oz macaroni

1 Cut the fish into fork-friendly chunks.

2 Bring 9½ cups cold water to a boil. Reduce the heat, add the fish chunks and a third of the parsley, and simmer for 10 minutes. Transfer the fish to a plate using a slotted spoon, and strain and reserve the cooking liquid.

3 Combine the olive oil, onion, garlic, tomatoes and half the remaining parsley in a clean saucepan. Season with salt and pepper and simmer gently for 10 minutes.

4 Add the fish broth and macaroni and cook gently until the pasta is done. Add the fish and heat through briefly. Sprinkle with the remaining parsley and serve hot.

miniature omelets with ricotta
frittatine con ricotta

These versatile little omelets, stuffed here with ricotta, make an impressive snack or a light meal – Sunday supper perhaps. Keep them whole, or cut them at an angle, and serve on some salad leaves. Once you have made them a few times, you will have the confidence to vary the filling. Even if you think you have nothing in the *dispensa* or pantry, you will find something that will work!

serves 4

8 large eggs

2 tbsp water

sea salt and freshly ground
 black pepper

a handful of fresh flat-leaf
 parsley, finely chopped

a handful of fresh mint leaves,
 finely chopped

1 garlic clove, peeled and finely
 chopped

1¼ cups Parmesan cheese,
 freshly grated

2-3 tbsp olive oil

filling

14 oz ricotta cheese

6 ripe tomatoes, seeded and
 finely chopped

a handful of fresh basil, torn

½ cup Parmesan cheese,
 freshly grated

1 In a bowl beat the eggs with the water, some salt and pepper, most of the parsley, and all the mint, garlic and cheese.

2 Heat a large, heavy-based frying pan with a little of the oil – the heat should be about medium. When the oil is hot, add a ladleful of the egg mixture: enough to produce a thin pancake. Reduce the heat and cook the miniature omelet until just firm. Flip it over and cook the other side. Keep warm. Continue in this way to make eight *frittatine*.

3 Make the filling by combining the ricotta, tomatoes, basil, Parmesan and some salt and pepper. Divide the mixture between the *frittatine*, roll up loosely and keep warm. Garnish with the remaining parsley.

grilled smoked mozzarella, radicchio and pancetta

carabiniere a cavallo

This dish translates as "mounted policeman", so named because the color and the fan shape of the radicchio looks like a *carabiniere's* hat.

serves 4

2 medium heads radicchio

1 tbsp olive oil

8 slices pancetta

4 thick slices smoked mozzarella
  (scamorza)

2 tbsp fruity extra virgin olive oil

**sea salt and freshly ground black
  pepper**

1 Rinse the radicchio and pat it dry. Cut in quarters. Do not trim the stem as it helps hold the leaves together.

2 Preheat a ridged cast-iron grill pan for 5 minutes. Brush the radicchio with olive oil and place on the grill. Add the pancetta slices and grill together for about 3 minutes on each side, or until the radicchio is tender. (This allows the radicchio to absorb the smoked aroma of the pancetta.) Remove from the grill pan.

3 Raise the temperature of the grill. Grill the mozzarella slices briefly, until grill marks appear on the surface.

4 On individual plates, fan two of the radicchio quarters. Top with two pancetta slices and one of grilled cheese. Drizzle with good oil and season with salt and pepper.

carpaccio with arugula and parmesan
carpaccio con rucola e parmigiano

Carpaccio was created by the restaurateur Giuseppe Cipriani, owner of Harry's Bar in Venice, in response to a request by a frequent guest whose doctor had recommended a special diet that included raw meat. Mr Cipriani came up with the idea of slicing a raw filet of beef paper-thin, like prosciutto, and sprinkling it with flavored mayonnaise. The dish is named after the great Renaissance painter, Carpaccio.

serves 4

1lb 10 oz beef filet, in one
  piece
9 oz arugula, rinsed
shavings of fresh Parmesan
(plenty)
4-6 tbsp extra virgin olive oil
sea salt and freshly ground black
  pepper
2 unwaxed lemons, halved

1 Wrap the beef in plastic wrap and place in the freezer for 2 hours. Remove the plastic wrap and, using a very sharp butcher's knife, cut the meat into paper-thin slices.

2 Cover four individual plates with the carpaccio slices. Top each plate with one-quarter of the arugula and Parmesan shavings. Drizzle with olive oil, season with salt and pepper and serve with half a lemon on the side.

carpaccio with gorgonzola and walnuts
carpaccio con gorgonzola e noci

This is my improvisation on the classic recipe. Carpaccio is a favorite in Italian *trattorias* – it involves only a few, but prime, ingredients, and it is incredibly easy to prepare.

serves 4

1lb 10 oz beef filet, in one
 piece
9 oz arugula, rinsed
9 oz aged *piccante* Gorgonzola,
 crumbled
¾ cup shelled fresh walnuts,
 coarsely chopped
a handful of fresh flat-leaf
 parsley, roughly chopped
4-6 tbsp extra virgin olive oil
sea salt and ground black pepper
2 unwaxed lemons, halved

1 Wrap the beef in plastic wrap and place in the freezer for 2 hours (this makes it easier to slice). Remove the plastic wrap and, using a very sharp butcher's knife, cut it into paper-thin slices.

2 Cover four individual plates with the carpaccio slices. Place a mound of arugula on top, and sprinkle on the cheese, walnuts and parsley. Drizzle with olive oil, season with salt and pepper, and serve with half a lemon on the side.

This recipe celebrates the young pecorino, which is gloriously sweet, and goes magnificently with the acidity of the onion marmalade. I enjoyed it at *Buca San Petronio*, a modern trattoria in central Bologna run by a young couple called Giorgio and Antonia Fini. I loved it, as I did the incredibly memorable pasta served with four wild herbs that followed.

bruschetta with caramelized red onion and young pecorino

bruschetta con marmellata di cipolle rosse e pecorino

serves 4

3 tbsp fruity extra virgin olive oil, plus extra for serving

3 red onions, peeled and chopped

2 bay leaves

1 sprig fresh rosemary, leaves picked from the stalks

2 tbsp red wine vinegar

¼ cup (packed) soft brown sugar

4 slices country bread, open textured, with a firm crust

4 handfuls mixed salad leaves

sea salt and freshly ground black pepper

4½ oz young pecorino

1 Heat 2 tbsp of the olive oil, then add the onions, bay and rosemary. Brown the onions well over low-to-medium heat, stirring regularly. Add the vinegar and stir well. Add the sugar and cook over low heat for 30 minutes. The mixture should be thick, shiny and rich red. Leave to cool.

2 Heat a ridged cast-iron grill pan until hot. Add the bread slices and cook for 1-2 minutes on each side, until lightly toasted and charred at the edges. Put the salad leaves in a bowl and add 1 tbsp olive oil and seasoning to taste. Toss.

3 To serve, spread 1 tbsp of the red onion mixture on each piece of toast and put on to serving plates. Add a handful of leaves and crumble the pecorino on top. Sprinkle with more olive oil and some black pepper.

crostini with roasted vegetables and mozzarella

crostini con verdure arrosto e mozzarella

In most *trattorias* throughout Italy, the bread oven is on permanently, so bread in some form or other will be on offer – plain to accompany the meal, or baked as crostini and topped with some speciality *della casa*.

serves 6

1 x 2-oz can oil-marinated
  anchovies
1 tbsp extra virgin olive oil
1 small, thin, tender zucchini,
  diced into ½-inch pieces
1 small yellow pepper, seeded and
  diced into ½-inch pieces
1 small eggplant, diced into
  ½-inch pieces
1 small red onion, halved and
  sliced through the root into
  half moons
12 cherry tomatoes, skinned
1 garlic clove, peeled and chopped
sea salt and freshly ground black
  pepper
12 thin slices ciabatta bread
10½ oz mozzarella,
  sliced into 12 pieces
6 large fresh basil leaves, roughly
  torn

1 Preheat the oven to 400°F.

2 Drain the can of anchovies, reserving the oil. Mix this with the extra virgin olive oil. Snip the anchovies into small pieces or leave them whole, whichever you prefer.

3 Place the diced vegetables, onion and tomatoes on a shallow heavy-duty baking tray and add the garlic. Season and drizzle the oil over. Make sure everything gets a good coating. Place on a high shelf in the oven for 30 minutes, or until toasted at the edges, then remove from the oven.

4 Place the bread slices on an oven tray and bake at the same temperature for 10 minutes. Remove the bread from the oven and turn the grill on to high. Cut the cheese to fit the bread slices as closely as possible and place on the baked bread. Grill for 2 minutes, until the cheese is just soft.

5 Divide the roasted vegetables and anchovies between the crostini, pressing lightly into the cheese, and grill for a further 3 minutes, until the cheese just begins to bubble. Garnish with basil and black pepper.

crostini with tapenade
crostini con tapenade

Small pieces of baked bread are topped with delicious things and served as appetite-whetters in *trattorias* all over Italy, but particularly in Umbria and Tuscany, which is where I got this idea. Tapenade is associated with Provence, but politically and culinarily, this region and northern Italy were very close at one point, and many recipes are similar. This tapenade topping is my own, with some ground almonds adding a slightly different taste and texture.

serves 6

6 slices day-old coarse-textured
  bread

3 tbsp fine extra virgin olive oil

tapenade

7 oz pitted, good-quality
  black olives

12 sun-dried tomatoes with 2 tbsp
of oil

a handful of fresh basil leaves

1 garlic clove, peeled

2 oz oil-marinated anchovies

2 oz salted capers, rinsed and
  dried

1 tbsp ground almonds

freshly ground black pepper

1 Place all the tapenade ingredients in a food processor and blend together to a coarse paste. This mixture may be kept in the refrigerator for several days and will get stronger and better.

2 Grill the bread until golden. Brush with oil and top with tapenade just before serving.

chicken livers on toast
crostini di fegatini di pollo

In Tuscany they eat an enormous amount of chicken, and this is just one of the many dishes made with chicken livers. Served hot with a glass of wine, it makes a delicious appetizer. This dish can be prepared in advance and reheated just before serving. It is based on a recipe from *Trattoria Rosa in the Via dei Tavolini* in Florence. I've hosted many a family gathering there, as the atmosphere is charming, the food is wonderful.

serves 4

4 chicken livers, trimmed and
  finely chopped

1 tbsp butter

1 tbsp chopped fresh flat-leaf
parsley

1 level tsp all-purpose flour

4 oil-marinated anchovy fillets,
  chopped

⅔ cup chicken broth (see
  page 253)

sea salt and freshly ground black
  pepper

a squeeze of lemon juice

2 tbsp freshly grated Parmesan

8–12 small pieces freshly made
  toast or fried bread

1 Fry the chicken livers in the butter until they are just brown. Stir in the parsley, flour and chopped anchovies. Add the broth and some salt and pepper (not too much salt), and cook down to a paste. This will take about 10 minutes.

2 Remove from the heat, then stir in the lemon juice and Parmesan. Spread on to hot toast or fried bread. Serve immediately.

salads & vegetables

artichoke and mushroom salad
insalata di carciofi e funghi

This is a wonderful combination of fresh, young, early summer vegetables and mushrooms, with contrasting colors, textures and flavors. It is easily prepared and assembled, and would make a great vegetable course, or indeed a light lunch with lots of crusty country bread.

serves 4

1 unwaxed lemon

18 oz baby artichokes

18 oz young white
  mushrooms

3 celery stalks, with leaves

12 oz baby spinach, washed
  and dried

7 oz arugula, washed, dried
  and stems removed

3½ oz Parmesan, cut into
  shavings

a handful of fresh chives, chopped

dressing

5 tbsp good-quality extra virgin
olive oil

2 tbsp balsamic vinegar

sea salt and freshly ground black
  pepper

1 Halve the lemon and then squeeze it into a medium bowl filled with water.

2 Remove the tough outer leaves from the artichokes and trim off the leaf tips. Cut each artichoke in half and cut out the choke with a small knife. Drop the artichoke halves into the acidulated water to prevent them from darkening.

3 Clean the mushrooms with a soft brush and trim the stems. Rinse the mushrooms quickly under cold running water. Gently pat dry with a paper towel. Slice the mushrooms ½-inch thick.

4 Remove the leaves from the celery stalks and reserve. Wash and slice the stalks thinly. Drain the artichokes and slice thinly with a very sharp knife.

5 On four serving plates, arrange a bed of spinach and arugula. Top with celery, mushrooms, Parmesan shavings and sliced artichoke.

6 In a bowl, whisk together the olive oil, balsamic vinegar and some salt and pepper. Drizzle the salad with the dressing and sprinkle with chopped chives and celery leaves.

This is typical of many *trattorias* in Sicily, where orange groves have been cultivated since the end of the 18th century. Since oranges are so abundant, locals combine them with seasonal vegetables to make salads.

fennel, endive and orange salad
insalata taormina

serves 4

2 medium fennel bulbs (both male and female preferably – see page 61), trimmed

4 heads Belgian endive (chicory)

3-4 oranges, fresh and in season

¾ cup shelled fresh walnuts, roughly chopped

2 tbsp olive tapenade (see page 34)

3 tbsp Sicilian extra virgin olive oil

juice of 1 unwaxed lemon

sea salt and freshly ground black pepper

1 Chop the fennel and cut the endive lengthwise into strips.

2 Using a sharp knife, cut the rinds off the oranges, removing all the white pith. Thinly slice the oranges crosswise.

3 On individual plates, arrange the orange, fennel and endive. Sprinkle with the walnuts.

4 In a small bowl, combine the olive tapenade with the olive oil and lemon juice. Drizzle over the salad and season with salt and pepper.

beef, potato, red onion and parsley salad
insalata toscana

The peasants of Tuscany have created many memorable dishes from leftovers, among them this delicious and hearty salad that has become a menu staple in many an Italian *trattoria*. This mixture of cubed beef and boiled potatoes, enlivened with some fresh parsley and oil, is a good example of authentic regional cuisine.

serves 6

18 oz brisket of beef

4 cups beef broth (see page 254)

2 cups red wine

½ onion, peeled and chopped

1 carrot, peeled and sliced

1 celery stalk, roughly sliced

1 bay leaf

6 medium Italian new potatoes

sea salt and freshly ground black pepper

4 tbsp Tuscan olive oil

3-4 fresh sage leaves

1 tbsp red wine vinegar

½ tsp dried chili (*peperoncino*)

1 red onion, peeled and coarsely chopped

2 plum tomatoes, skinned and finely diced

a handful of fresh flat-leaf parsley, chopped

1 Place the meat in a large saucepan with the beef broth, wine, onion, carrot, celery and bay leaf. Bring to a boil over high heat, then reduce the heat to medium. Cover and simmer for 2 hours.

2 Drain the meat (saving the stock for another dish, a soup perhaps). When cool enough to handle, cut the meat into ¾-inch cubes and set aside.

3 Meanwhile scrub, peel and dice the potatoes. Place in a saucepan with 3½ cups salted water, 2 tsp of the olive oil and the sage leaves. Bring to a boil and simmer for 5 minutes. Drain and set aside.

4 In a small bowl, whisk together the remaining olive oil, the vinegar, some salt and pepper and the chili.

5 In a large bowl combine the meat, diced potatoes, red onion, tomatoes and chopped parsley. Add the dressing and toss well.

renaissance chicken salad
insalata isabella

In 1489, this recipe was served to 500 guests at the wedding banquet of Isabel of Aragon to Giano Galeazzo Sforza, an Italian nobleman. It is still a most elegant dish. At that time capon was used instead of chicken. I got the recipe from the *Trattoria Vernaccia* in Florence, which is on the Via dei Tavolini (most appropriately, the "road of the tables"!) They make their own bread there, and serve their own wine from vineyards in Chianti.

serves 6

3lb chicken

1 carrot, peeled

1 onion, peeled

2 celery stalks

1 bunch fresh flat-leaf parsley

2 garlic cloves, peeled

4-5 whole black peppercorns

sea salt and freshly ground black
  pepper

salad

⅔ cup fine extra virgin
  olive oil

juice of 2 lemons

½ cup (packed) raisins

2 small apples

1 whole celery, trimmed

1 small fennel bulb, trimmed

5 tbsp salted capers

2 frisée lettuces, washed and
  trimmed

1 To cook the chicken, place in a large casserole dish with the carrot, onion, celery, parsley, garlic, peppercorns, 1 tsp salt and water to just cover. Bring to a boil, covered, then reduce the heat and simmer gently for 1 hour, until the chicken is cooked. Remove the chicken to a plate and cool. Discard the skin and bones and cut the meat into strips.

2 To start the salad, combine 6 tbsp of the olive oil and the juice of 1½ lemons in a mixing bowl. Add the chicken, toss, and chill for 2 hours.

3 Soak the raisins in tepid water for 30 minutes. Meanwhile, peel and core the apples and cut into thin slices. Slice the celery and fennel thinly. In another bowl, soak the capers in tepid water for 20 minutes.

4 Just before serving, drain the raisins and capers and toss with the chicken. Add the apples, celery and fennel. Whisk together the remaining olive oil and lemon juice, season with salt and pepper, and toss with the salad.

5 Make beds of frisée leaves on six plates. Top with the chicken salad and serve immediately.

salad of apple, speck and asiago cheese
insalata jacopo da pontormo

Jacopo da Pontormo was a Renaissance painter who kept a journal of his gastronomic experiments. This recipe is a modern variation of one of his recipes. Speck is a kind of smoked prosciutto available in the northern regions of Italy; if you can't find it, substitute regular Parma ham.

serves 4

1 red apple
9 oz speck or Parma ham
9 oz *Asiago* cheese
1 frisée lettuce and 1 bunch mache, washed and trimmed
sea salt and ground black pepper

lemon dressing
6 tbsp extra virgin olive oil
finely grated zest and juice of 1 unwaxed lemon

1 In a small bowl whisk together the olive oil, lemon juice and lemon zest.

2 Core the unpeeled apple and slice very thinly. Cut the speck into thin strips. Cut the cheese into small cubes.

3 In a serving bowl, combine the frisée and mache with the apple, speck and cheese. Toss well with the lemon dressing and season with salt and pepper to taste.

This recipe is Sicilian in essence, the use of pine nuts and pomegranate betraying the Arab influence on Sicily's cooking. Pomegranates are beautiful to look at and just as good to eat, but it is very time-consuming to pick the edible seeds, impacted like teeth in a white membrane, from the inside of the fruit. Each tiny tart and sweet, juicy, garnet-colored seed is encased in a thin-skinned transparent covering, and they look like jewels. Pomegranate seeds are delicious sprinkled on salads, fruit dishes and ice-creams. You can pass the seeds through a food mill to drink the refreshing liquid – and indeed pomegranate juice is used to tenderize meat!

arugula with pine nuts and pomegranate

rucola con pinoli e melograno

serves 6

**2 bunches (approx. 10½ oz)
  arugula leaves (the wild variety is
  best), washed and dried**

1 cup pine nuts

1 cup fresh pomegranate seeds

dressing

2 tbsp red wine vinegar

1 tsp any mustard (optional)

1 shallot, peeled and minced

2 anchovies, crushed

2 tbsp extra virgin olive oil

sea salt and ground black pepper

1 Put the arugula into a large bowl. Toast the pine nuts under the grill or in a hot frying pan, tossing the pan very regularly to prevent burning.

2 To make the dressing, put the vinegar, mustard (if using), minced shallot and crushed anchovies into a small bowl and whisk together. Add the oil drop by drop. Season with salt and pepper.

3 Sprinkle the toasted pine nuts and half the pomegranate seeds over the arugula and pour the dressing over the salad. Gently toss. Sprinkle with the remaining pomegranate seeds.

salad of anchovies, peppers and walnuts
acciughe con peperoni e noci

Many *trattorias* and many homes would serve a salad like this at lunch or dinner. In Calabria, this is often served as a first course on its own or with a shellfish salad or a few stuffed squid.

serves 4

3 red or yellow peppers

10 anchovy fillets (best in oil)

4 hard-boiled eggs, shelled and halved

½ cup shelled walnuts, roughly chopped

1 tbsp capers

a handful of arugula leaves

extra virgin fruity olive oil

sea salt and freshly ground black pepper

1 Grill the peppers under a hot grill until the skins are blackened and puffed. Remove the papery outside of the skins if you wish, while running them under a cold tap. Cut the peppers into halves and remove the cores.

2 Lay the peppers on the bottom of a shallow dish, cover with the anchovy fillets, then the halved hard-boiled eggs, then the walnuts, then the capers and finally the arugula. Drizzle with the oil and season to taste.

frisée, caciotta cheese, pancetta and poached egg salad
insalata chiantigiana

During harvest time in the Chianti region, peasants have spent long hours in the vineyards. To lighten their day, the women prepared this appealing and simple cold salad which features *caciotta*, a mild sheep's milk cheese. A similar tradition exists in France in the Beaujolais region. I have added the poached egg to enhance the flavors and give it a sunny touch.

serves 4

10½ oz pancetta, cut into
  strips

2-3 tbsp extra virgin olive oil

1 tbsp balsamic vinegar

sea salt and freshly ground black
  pepper

1 frisée lettuce, washed, dried
  and separated into leaves

4 large eggs

10½ oz *caciotta* cheese, grated into
shavings

a handful of croutons

1   In a frying pan, cook the pancetta slowly over medium
heat until it is crisp. Drain on paper towels.

2   In a large bowl, whisk together the oil, vinegar and some
salt and pepper to taste. Add the frisée and toss well.

3   Bring a shallow pan of water to a simmer. Crack the eggs,
carefully slide them into the water and poach for 3 minutes.

4   While the eggs poach, arrange the dressed frisée on four
serving plates. Place a poached egg in the center of each
and surround it with some cheese, pancetta and croutons.

artichoke, zucchini and asparagus tart
torta di carciofi, zucchini e asparagi

Vegetable tarts are classic *trattoria* fare, and are also ideal for quick
meals at home. This would be perfect for brunch, for instance, as it is
really tasty and simple. Ring the changes with different combinations of
vegetables. The pastry is an Italian classic.

serves 4-6

⅔ cup unsalted butter

1½ cups all-purpose flour

4 tbsp ice water

a pinch of salt

filling

7 oz young tender asparagus, cut
   into 1-inch pieces at an angle

2-3 tbsp olive oil

4 young zucchini, thinly sliced
   at an angle

1 x 6-oz jar artichoke hearts in
   oil, cut into quarters

2 medium garlic cloves, peeled
   and finely chopped

a handful of fresh basil leaves, torn

2 large eggs, beaten

2 cups Parmesan cheese,
   freshly grated

sea salt and freshly ground black
   pepper

1 Place the butter, flour, water and salt in a food processor
   and pulse until a dough forms. Wrap the pastry in plastic
   wrap and chill in the refrigerator for 45 minutes.

2 Preheat the oven to 400°F.

3 To start the filling, spread the asparagus over a baking
   sheet and sprinkle with 1 tbsp of the olive oil. Roast for 6
   minutes, until softened but still *al dente*.

4 Fry the zucchini in the remaining oil until golden.
   Combine with the asparagus and all the remaining filling
   ingredients, seasoning to taste.

5 Roll out the pastry until it is ½-inch thick and roughly
   14-inch square. Use to line your tart pan. Prick with a
   fork all over and freeze for 10 minutes until solid. Remove
   and put straight into the oven for 10 minutes, until only
   lightly golden. This ensures the pastry will not shrink
   and it won't have time to rise.

6 Spread the vegetable mixture evenly over the partially-
   baked pastry shell, and bake for 15 minutes, until golden.
   Cool and serve in squares or triangles, etc.

roman artichokes
carciofi alla romana

The Romans seem to celebrate the artichoke more than the people of any other region of Italy, preparing and cooking them in varying ways. In the markets of Lazio you see stallholders peeling, chopping and storing artichokes in acidulated water, ready for a customer's lunch. This recipe is one of my favorites, but then I am addicted to artichokes...

serves 4

4 medium artichokes, stalks cut
  at an angle
1 lemon, cut in half
3 fresh bay leaves
⅔ cup white wine

dressing

a very generous handful of fresh
  mint leaves
2 medium garlic cloves, peeled
3-4 tbsp extra virgin olive oil
2 tbsp white wine vinegar
sea salt and freshly ground black
  pepper

1 Peel one artichoke stem, then cut the top off the artichoke leaves – approximately ¼-inch from the top. Rub the cut artichoke with half the lemon. Start peeling the leaves off the artichoke – at least four layers – until a pale yellow is revealed. Cut the artichoke in half and remove the choke and the prickly purple leaves. Dip the artichoke into a bowl of cold water acidulated with the other half of the lemon. Repeat with the other artichokes.

2 In a large pan, place the bay leaves, lemon halves, wine and artichokes, and enough cold water to cover the artichokes. Season with salt, then boil for approximately 30-35 minutes, until tender. Drain well.

3 To make the dressing, finely chop the mint and garlic together on a board. Place in a bowl with the oil, vinegar and salt and pepper to taste.

4 Arrange the artichokes face down on serving plates and squash lightly so that the leaves fan out. The stalk will be sticking up. Pour over the dressing while still warm and serve.

artichoke bottoms braised in olive oil with garlic and mint

fondi di carciofo stufati in olio d'oliva

During their seasons, artichokes are enjoyed in Italy on an almost daily basis. The first crop comes in around March and April, followed by a second in September and October. This is another Roman recipe, one of the many, and it is made particularly delicious by the inclusion of fresh mint.

serves 4

4 large artichokes, with plenty of stem

2 lemons, halved

4¼ cups water

3 tbsp olive oil

3 garlic cloves, peeled and chopped

a handful of fresh mint, finely chopped

sea salt and freshly ground black pepper

1 Keep the stem attached and, at the opposite end, cut off the top 1 inch of an artichoke with a serrated knife. Bend back the outer leaves until they snap off close to the base, then discard more layers of leaves until you reach the pale yellow leaves with pale green tips. Cut the remaining leaves flush with the top of the artichoke bottom, using a sharp knife, then pull off the leaves and scoop out the fuzzy choke with a melon baller. Trim the dark green fibrous parts from the base and sides of the artichoke with a sharp paring knife. Rub the cut surfaces with a lemon half. Trim the remaining artichokes in the same manner.

2 Put the water and oil in a heavy-based pan to boil. Mince the garlic and half the mint with salt. Rub the garlic paste into the cavity of each artichoke, then stand the artichokes upside-down in the liquid in the pan. Sprinkle over salt and simmer over low heat, covered, for 20-30 minutes.

3 Transfer the artichokes to a serving dish and boil the cooking liquid, whisking it until emulsified and reduced to a third of its original volume. Pour this sauce over the artichokes and serve warm or at room temperature. Chop the remaining mint and use as a garnish.

baked stuffed zucchini
zucchine ripiene

Stuffed zucchini and other stuffed vegetables are a staple of *trattoria* and home cooking. They are prepared and cooked in advance, probably on a daily basis during the brief zucchini season. Try to get really big zucchini for this, because they are easier to handle.

serves 4

4 large zucchini, about
   3-4 inches wide and 10-12 inches
   long, scrubbed and washed, with
   stem ends cut off and saved

2¾ cups fresh breadcrumbs

3½ oz Parma ham
   (*prosciutto di Parma*), diced

⅔ cup pecorino, grated

⅔ cup Parmesan, grated

2 slices salami, diced

3 oz provolone, diced

a handful of fresh flat-leaf
   parsley, chopped

a handful of pine nuts

3 medium tomatoes, skinned,
   seeded and chopped

sea salt and freshly ground black
   pepper

olive oil

1 small onion, peeled and thinly
   sliced

⅓ cup dry white wine

¼ cup unsalted butter

1 With the thin blade of a sharp knife, remove the center pulp from each zucchini, working from the cut end, leaving an unbroken shell about ¼-inch thick. Discard the pulp.

2 Put the breadcrumbs in a large bowl and add all the ingredients in the ingredients list up to and including the tomatoes. Season, then add enough olive oil and a little water to make a stuffing that holds together but isn't wet.

3 Stuff each zucchini shell with stuffing, pushing it inside with your fingers and a wooden spoon end. Replace the end pieces, securing them with wooden toothpicks.

4 Preheat the oven to 300°F. Pour enough oil into a frying pan to just cover the bottom, heat, then add the zucchini. Gently cook and roll until golden brown all over. Transfer to a lightly oiled shallow baking dish. In the same pan, cook the onion until golden, then add the wine, butter, salt and pepper. Stir and cook for 1 minute. Pour over the zucchini and bake for 45 minutes.

5 Remove the zucchini and let them cool. When ready to serve, remove the toothpicks and end pieces and discard. Cut each zucchini into small slices and arrange in a clean baking dish. Spoon the sauce over and serve.

braised fennel with pecorino
finocchio brasato con pecorino

Every *trattoria* in Italy relies on fresh seasonal produce, and fennel
features prominently in the winter, because it is at its best and most
juicy around Christmas. The Italians love fennel, both for its flavor and
for its alkalinity, which they feel is helpful in the diet. This would be
served as a *contorno*, a vegetable dish on its own, and would be perfect
after a heavy meat or fish dish. Experiment with the recipe – you could
try using Gorgonzola instead of the pecorino, for instance.

serves 4

1 male fennel bulb (long and
   thin, no hips)
1 female fennel bulb (bulbous
   and hippy)
sea salt and freshly ground black
   pepper
1¼ tbsp unsalted butter
1 tbsp olive oil
5½ oz pecorino, in shavings

1   Slice each well washed fennel bulb vertically into two
    pieces, keeping any fronds for garnish. Blanch in boiling
    salted water for 5 minutes, then drain well.

2   Melt the butter and oil in a heavy-based pan over
    medium heat, then braise the fennel pieces for 10-12
    minutes, turning them over in the pan. Both sides should
    be brown. Season with salt and pepper in the pan.

3   Transfer to a serving platter, sprinkle with pecorino
    shavings and garnish with fennel fronds.

mushroom pancakes
soffiatine

These crepes could be served as the equivalent of the pasta course in a *trattoria*, but are wonderful as a light lunch. As with foods such as fish baked in parchment paper, there is an element of surprise when a filling is encased in a pancake. This mushroom filling is classically Italian, but you can vary the ingredients as you like.

serves 6

⅔ cup all-purpose flour

⅔ cup whole milk

2 large eggs, beaten

⅓ cup unsalted butter, melted

freshly grated Parmesan cheese

filling

¼ cup unsalted butter

2 shallots, peeled and finely
  chopped

1 garlic clove, peeled and crushed

13 oz field mushrooms,
  wiped and sliced

4½ oz mixed wild
  mushrooms, cleaned and sliced

8 oz mozzarella, diced

¾ cup Parmesan, grated

8 oz ricotta

a handful of fresh basil, torn

sea salt and freshly ground black
  pepper

1 To make the filling, melt the butter in a large frying pan, add the shallots, garlic and both kinds of mushrooms, and sauté until golden, stirring constantly. In a medium mixing bowl, combine the mushroom mixture with the remaining filling ingredients, season to taste and set aside.

2 Preheat the oven to 350°F.

3 To make the crepes, mix the flour and milk in a bowl. Add the eggs and a pinch of salt and whisk. Pass the batter through a sieve. Brush a 12-inch round heavy-based frying pan with melted butter and set over moderate heat. Pour a small ladleful of the batter into the pan and make a thin pancake. Repeat with the remaining butter and batter. When cooked on both sides, stack each crepe on a plate.

4 Put a spoonful of the filling in the center of each pancake and fold over two edges to meet in the center, then fold over the other two edges making a parcel. Place on a greased, high-sided baking tray, joins down. Brush with the remaining melted butter and sprinkle with Parmesan to taste. Bake in the preheated oven for 10-15 minutes. Serve immediately.

potato cake

torta di patate

There are numerous variations of this potato cake, a basic in many a *trattoria*, but this is my family's favorite. We serve it at picnics in the countryside accompanied by red wine, and followed by fruit. It could be served as a vegetable side dish, or as a vegetable course.

serves 6-8

3lb Russet Burbank or Idaho
  potatoes,
  peeled and quartered
sea salt and freshly ground black
  pepper
4 large eggs
1 cup milk
2 garlic cloves, peeled and
  crushed
¾ cup unsalted butter
7 oz Parmesan, grated
6 slices salami, chopped
3½ oz *Caciocavallo* or
  provolone cheese, diced
5½ oz mozzarella, diced
a handful of fresh flat-leaf
  parsley, chopped
6 oz pancetta, diced
1 cup dried breadcrumbs

1 Preheat the oven to 375°F. Cook the potatoes in lightly salted boiling water until tender – about 15 minutes. Drain. Pass through a food mill or ricer into a large bowl and leave to cool.

2 Add the eggs, milk, garlic, most of the butter, and all the other ingredients except the pancetta and breadcrumbs to the potato. Stir around until everything is well mixed. Season to taste.

3 In a hot frying pan, cook the pancetta cubes until golden and then mix into the potato mixture.

4 Grease the bottom and sides of a 10-inch round cake pan, with at least 3-inch sides, with the reserved butter. Coat with about three-quarters of the breadcrumbs. Turn the potato mixture into the pan and smooth down evenly. Sprinkle lightly with the remaining breadcrumbs and press into the potato mixture.

5 Bake for 45 minutes. Let it rest for 5 minutes, then pass the blade of a knife round the sides of the pan. Put a round plate several inches larger than the pan over it and, holding both securely, invert the pan. The cake will slide out on to the plate. Serve hot or cold.

trattoria di montagliari

Trattorias in Tuscany have remained true to their traditional style, despite the tourist invasion and the region's re-christening as "Chiantishire." Checked cloths and candles on the tables are still the norm, most *trattorias* are family-run, and they are basic and unfussy.

In late summer, a Tuscan speciality might be the much-prized *ovolo*, which is otherwise known as Caesar's mushroom. But the majority of Tuscan *trattorias* are most proud of their good meaty dishes, for the land is geared to livestock as well as to vegetable and fruit farming. Another influence on the food must be the weather, for in winter Tuscany can be wickedly cold, so dishes must be warming and sustaining.

The *Trattoria di Montagliari*, which was Mario and Fiammetta when I visited, is typical of the region's *trattorias*. Set in beautiful surroundings, next to a working farm growing mostly olives and vines, it is a wonderful home-away-from-home in the best *trattoria* tradition, offering straightforward cooking that uses the finest ingredients.

mixed vegetable casserole

canazzo

The Italian name translates as "big dog," and this is a typical vegetable dish served in *trattorias* during the winter. It comes to the table steaming hot, and every morsel is devoured with relish. Eat it with bread to mop up the fragrant juices, and don't forget *la scarpetta*, the last piece of bread that wipes the bowl clean, so clean that it doesn't look as though it has been used!

serves 4

1 medium eggplant, cut into
  1-inch cubes

sea salt and freshly ground black
  pepper

3 tbsp olive oil

1 large onion, peeled and chopped

1 x 14.50-oz can diced tomatoes

2 red peppers, cored, seeded and
  sliced

2 yellow peppers, cored, seeded
  and sliced

14 oz Italian old potatoes
  (Spunta), peeled and cut into
  1-inch cubes

a handful of fresh flat-leaf
  parsley, chopped

1 Put the eggplant cubes into a colander, sprinkle with salt and leave to "degorge" for 20 minutes. Rinse and dry.

2 Heat half the oil in a large saucepan, add the onion and cook for 5 minutes. Add the tomatoes and their juices and a pinch of salt, and simmer for 10 minutes.

3 In the remaining olive oil, fry the eggplant in batches until golden brown. Drain on paper towels.

4 Add the peppers to the pan of tomatoes and cook for a further 5 minutes, then add the potatoes, mix well and simmer for another 15 minutes, or until the potatoes are tender. Add the eggplant and parsley and heat through briefly. Adjust the seasoning.

gratin of mushrooms with pancetta
funghi gratinati con pancetta

This is the sort of recipe you would find in a Tuscan *trattoria* in the autumn. Tuscany is a haven for fungi hunters, especially those looking for ceps (the famous Italian *funghi porcini*). If you were lucky enough to find some of these – either in the wild, or in the shops – this simple recipe would be perfect.

serves 6

1 tbsp olive oil

½ cup unsalted butter

5½ oz diced pancetta

2¼lb mushrooms (field, Portobello or chestnut, or a combination), cleaned and cut into thick slices

sea salt and freshly ground black pepper

2 garlic cloves, peeled and crushed

1 cup Parmesan, grated

1 cup pecorino, grated

4 tomatoes, seeded and chopped

2 medium onions, peeled and thinly sliced, rings separated

a handful of fresh flat-leaf parsley, finely chopped

a handful of fresh white breadcrumbs

1   Preheat the oven to 350°F. Grease a shallow baking dish about 9 x 14 inches with the olive oil and 1 tbsp of the butter.

2   Heat a medium frying pan and fry the pancetta dice until golden brown.

3   Arrange half the mushrooms over the bottom of the prepared dish, season well and add half the crushed garlic. Sprinkle over half the two cheeses, and half the pancetta, tomatoes, onions and parsley.

4   Make another layer of mushrooms, garlic, cheeses, pancetta, tomatoes, onion and parsley. Season well. Spread the breadcrumbs on top and dot with the remaining butter.

5   Bake for 30 minutes and serve hot.

baked celery with pancetta

sedano al forno con pancetta

This is a truly great way to serve celery as a vegetable, whether as a side dish, as a *contorno* or vegetable course, or perhaps even as an appetizer. Wax or parchment paper is ideal, as it looks very attractive when you take the "parcel" to the table.

serves 4

2 whole celery

12 shallots

3 tbsp olive oil

6 slices pancetta

2 garlic cloves, peeled

4 sprigs fresh thyme

4 small sprigs fresh rosemary

4 fresh sage leaves

sea salt and freshly ground black
   pepper

2 tsp white wine vinegar

1 Preheat the oven to 400°F. Remove the tough outer layers from the celery, then trim the root but leave the base attached. Now cut across the celery about 3½ inches from the base, then stand the lower half upright and cut in half vertically through the center. Cut each half into four to make eight pieces, keeping them attached to the base. Wash. Peel the shallots. If bulbs divide, split them.

2 Heat 2 tbsp of the olive oil in a frying pan, then lightly brown the celery and shallots. Keep them moving so they brown evenly. Transfer them to a plate. Increase the heat, add the pancetta and garlic and fry for 2-3 minutes.

3 Lay four large sheets of parchment paper over an oven tray and lightly grease a 9-inch circle on each. Arrange the celery on the paper, putting the prettiest pieces on the top. Add the shallots, thyme, rosemary and sage, and season.

4 Combine the remaining olive oil with the vinegar and sprinkle all over the vegetables, followed by the pancetta. Fold the paper over and seal each parcel (it is important to keep steam trapped inside). Bake for 40 minutes. Unwrap the paper packages on plates at the table. Serve

This comes from Claudio Brugalossi of *La Taverna* in Perugia, a delightful *trattoria* which serves very good, simple food. It is a family recipe, and employs three cooking methods: boiling, sautéing and roasting. The major difference from other potato recipes is the use of breadcrumbs. This is very typically Italian – waste nothing, not even stale bread – and adds a delightful crunch.

crispy roasted potatoes
patate arrosto

serves 4

2lb Russet Burbank, Idaho or Red
  potatoes, peeled
  and cut into 1 x 1½-inch
  chunks

sea salt and freshly ground black
  pepper

1¾ tbsp unsalted butter

2 tbsp olive oil

2 generous sprigs fresh rosemary,
  finely chopped

1 tbsp fine dried breadcrumbs

1 Preheat the oven to 400°F.

2 Put the potatoes in a large pan and fill it with cold water to cover them by 2 inches. Bring to a boil, add a good pinch of salt and boil for 2 minutes. Drain the potatoes.

3 Combine the butter, olive oil and rosemary in a large ovenproof pan that will hold the potatoes comfortably in a single layer. Heat over medium-to-high heat and, when the butter has melted, add the potatoes and sauté them, tossing frequently, until they begin to brown. Season with salt and pepper, sprinkle with breadcrumbs and toss.

4 Transfer the pan to the center shelf of the oven and roast for 20-30 minutes, tossing occasionally, until the potatoes are crusty on the outside and creamy on the inside. Serve immediately with any meat or fish dish.

fava beans and swiss chard stewed with wine and tomato

scafata

Scafata is an Umbrian speciality, and it is a wonderfully tasty dish to make in the early summer, when fava beans and Swiss chard are in season. This recipe was inspired by the *Spante* near Orvieto, an *agriturismo* that is run by the Faina family, and where the grandmother is still in charge! It is a magical place, situated near the ancient Etruscan settlement of Volsinii. Swiss chard is becoming more readily available now, and it complements the familiar friends – fava beans and bacon – to perfection.

serves 6

4lb fresh fava beans in
   the pod, or 1lb 9 oz frozen

1 dried chili (*peperoncini*)

4 oz diced pancetta

1 small carrot, peeled

1 onion, peeled

1 celery stalk

1 sprig fresh rosemary

2 tbsp extra virgin olive oil

⅔ cup dry white wine

8 oz tomato sauce

sea salt and freshly ground black
   pepper

1lb Swiss chard (or spinach)

1 Pod the fresh fava beans or thaw the frozen ones. Put the chili in a bowl and cover with hot water to soften.

2 Now make the *battuto* (chopped mixture). Finely chop the pancetta, carrot, onion, celery, rosemary and drained chili. Put the mixture into a heavy-based pan with the oil and sauté gently for 10 minutes. Add the fava beans and wine and bring to a boil. Now add the tomato sauce and some salt, cover, then cook for 35 minutes. Add some water if it gets too dry.

3 Wash the Swiss chard and remove the green leaves from the white stalks (keep these for another dish). Cut the leaves into ½-inch strips. Pack them into the fava bean pan and, as soon as they have wilted, turn them over to mingle with the beans. When the mixture comes back to a boil, cover and cook for half an hour longer, stirring occasionally and adding a little boiling water whenever necessary. Check the seasoning. Serve hot.

italian flat romano bean salad with mint
insalata di fagiolini romani

Italian flat Romano beans are rarely found outside Italy, but if you can't get them green beans will do just as well. Romano beans are eaten in the pod, which is the dark green of fava beans, but are flatter, like runner beans, and smooth on the outside. Just harvested, green and gold, the beans are delightful served cold (which means at room temperature in Italy).

serves 4

1½lb green and gold flat
  Romano beans in the pod, or any
  similar green beans
1 small tomato, cut into wedges
fresh mint sprigs

dressing
6 tbsp extra virgin olive oil
2 tbsp red wine vinegar
1 garlic clove, peeled and sliced
sea salt
2 tbsp chopped mint leaves

1 To make the dressing, combine the olive oil, vinegar, garlic and a pinch of salt in a small bowl. Whisk together and allow to stand for 1 hour.

2 Trim the beans and cut them into 2-inch lengths. Fill a large pan with water and bring it to a boil. Add salt to taste. Stir in the beans and boil for 5-10 minutes, or just until tender. Drain in a colander, refresh under cold water and drain again. Transfer to a serving bowl.

3 Stir the chopped mint into the dressing, pour it on to the beans and toss until thoroughly coated. Garnish with tomato wedges and mint sprigs.

milanese-style fennel

finocchio alla milanese

A dish such as this would be staple fare on many a *trattoria* menu in the winter months, when fennel is at its best. The recipe is based on a dish from Lalla Morassutti of *Trattoria Mendola* in Milan. I was taken there on a business trip, and was eager to return the next day to enjoy the homey atmosphere and delicious food again. The dish can be served as a *contorno* or vegetable course by itself, or it goes well with simple fish dishes. It can be made a day ahead of serving, then reheated when required.

serves 6

2 large fennel bulbs, male and
    female (see page 61), trimmed
    and cut into ½-inch strips
sea salt and freshly ground black
    pepper

sauce

1¾ tbsp unsalted butter
2 tbsp all-purpose flour
1½ cups whole milk
½ tsp freshly grated nutmeg

topping

½ cup dried breadcrumbs
3 tbsp freshly grated Parmesan
1¾ tbsp unsalted butter, melted
paprika for garnish

1 Preheat the oven to 400°F.

2 Boil the fennel for 4 minutes in plenty of salted water. Drain and set aside.

3 To make the sauce, melt the butter in a saucepan, add the flour and cook for 1 minute. Remove from the heat and gradually stir in the milk. Cook over medium heat, stirring constantly, until the sauce boils and thickens. Add the nutmeg and season to taste with salt and pepper.

4 To make the topping, combine the breadcrumbs, Parmesan cheese and butter.

5 Arrange the fennel in a shallow ovenproof dish, pour the sauce over and sprinkle with the topping. Dust with paprika and bake in the preheated oven for 15-20 minutes, or until browned.

potato baskets with mushrooms
canestrini di patate con funghi

This recipe comes from the *Hotel Relais La Suvera*, near Siena. It is rather a grand hotel in the mountains, which is family owned and run, and has been so for more than 200 years. The patron, the Marchesa Eleonora Maria, spelled out the details of her delicious recipe.

serves 4

1½lb potatoes, peeled

sea salt and freshly ground black pepper

1¾ tbsp unsalted butter, softened

4 large egg yolks

½ tsp freshly grated nutmeg

3 tbsp all-purpose flour

2 large eggs, lightly beaten

⅔ cup fine dried breadcrumbs

sunflower oil for frying

mushroom filling

6 oz mixed mushrooms, preferably with some field, chestnut and fresh *porcini* (ceps)

2 tbsp olive oil

1 garlic clove, peeled

1 Place the potatoes in a large pan, cover with cold water and bring to a boil, adding salt to taste. Boil for 20-30 minutes, or until tender. Drain and purée through a ricer. Return to the pan and stir over medium heat to evaporate any moisture; the potatoes are dry when they begin to coat the bottom of the pan. Add the butter and stir until melted. Transfer to a large bowl and leave to cool.

2 When the potatoes are cool, stir in the egg yolks and nutmeg. Divide into eight equal portions. Roll each portion into a ball. Dredge the ball in flour and shake off the excess. Gently press the bottom of a shot glass into the center of each potato ball to flatten it and make a well in the center. Refrigerate the potato baskets until chilled and firm.

3 To prepare the mushroom filling, fully clean the mushrooms. Trim away the dry stalk ends and brush away any soil or dirt. Wipe the mushrooms with a damp cloth, then coarsely chop.

4 Heat the olive oil in a frying pan over medium heat. Add the garlic and cook
   until it is golden brown. Stir in the mushrooms and sauté until they are
   cooked through and any liquid in the pan has evaporated. Season to taste with
   salt and pepper and remove the clove of garlic.

5 When the potato baskets are firm, dip them one at a time into the lightly
   beaten egg, then coat them with breadcrumbs. Refrigerate until ready to fry.

6 Heat 1½-inches sunflower oil in a large heavy-based frying pan with high
   sides, over medium heat. When the oil is hot, add half of the potato baskets
   hollow-side-up. Fry, turning the baskets once, until they are golden brown.
   Using a slotted spoon, remove the baskets and keep warm. Fry the remaining
   baskets in the same way. Drain well.

7 Reheat the mushrooms, sprinkle the potato baskets with salt and fill the
   hollows with equal portions of mushroom. Serve immediately.

rice, pasta,
gnocchi & polenta

sautéed risotto cake
risotto al salto

This recipe is a great spin on risotto. Serve it as an *antipasto*, as I have had it in a *trattoria* in the Veneto.

serves 2

¼ cup unsalted butter

1 cup freshly cooked risotto
(you could use the recipe on
  page 84)

3 tbsp freshly grated Parmesan

freshly ground black pepper

1 In a medium frying pan melt the butter. Add the risotto to the pan and flatten with a spoon or fork into a ½-inch thick pancake. Sauté for 3-4 minutes until golden and a crust has formed.

2 Sprinkle the top with the grated Parmesan. Flip the pancake over with the help of a spatula and sauté for 3-4 minutes on the second side.

3 Cut into wedges and serve sprinkled with extra freshly grated Parmesan and some black pepper.

This is really a pantry risotto, one made at home using ingredients usually present in the Italian *dispensa*. You can use any risotto rice – arborio, carnaroli or vialone nano – but I prefer vialone nano, as the grains are shorter, and they cook more creamily. Always serve a risotto on warm plates, otherwise it will stick.

pancetta, sage and parmesan risotto
risotto con pancetta, salvia e parmigiano

serves 4

2 small onions or 8 shallots, peeled and finely chopped

5½ oz diced pancetta

⅔ cup unsalted butter

½ cup risotto rice

6⅓ cups hot chicken broth (see page 253)

6 medium sage leaves, chopped

1 cup Parmesan, grated

sea salt and freshly ground black pepper

1 In a pan melt ½ cup of the butter and then cook the onions and pancetta until soft – about 5 minutes.

2 Add the rice and stir for a minute while it fries lightly in the butter. Pour in a ladleful of hot broth and let the rice simmer, adding another ladle or two as the stock is absorbed. Add the sage. Cook, stirring continuously, until the broth is all used.

3 Stir in the remaining butter and all the Parmesan, plus some salt and pepper. The risotto should be "*al onda,*" like the waves in the sea. Remove from heat and cover for 4 minutes before serving.

rice croquettes
arancini di riso

This is my take on the traditional *arancini di riso* recipe, a popular finger food. Use any risotto for this recipe.

serves 4

1¼ cups freshly cooked risotto
(you could use the recipe on page
  84), cooled

3 tbsp all-purpose flour

3 large eggs, beaten

2¾ cups fresh breadcrumbs

5 tbsp olive oil

croquette stuffing

3 tbsp olive oil

1 garlic clove, peeled and chopped

½ onion, peeled and chopped

1 celery stalk, chopped

5½ oz minced veal

⅓ cup dry white wine

1 tbsp tomato paste

1¼ oz dried *porcini*, soaked for
  30 minutes, drained and diced

sea salt and freshly ground black
  pepper

3 oz fresh steamed peas

4½ oz mozzarella, cubed

a handful of fresh basil leaves, torn

1 To make the stuffing, in a pan heat the oil and sauté the garlic, onion, celery and veal over medium heat for 5-7 minutes, breaking the veal up with a wooden spoon, until golden brown. Add the wine and cook until it evaporates. Add the tomato paste and 7⅓ cups water, cover and cook over low heat for at least 1 hour, adding more water if necessary. Add the *porcini* and season.

2 In a bowl, mix the peas with the cubed mozzarella and torn basil. Set aside.

3 With your hands, mould the risotto into small spheres about the size of a tangerine. Cut the spheres in half with a teaspoon and scoop a well in the centre of each half. Fill one half with some meat mixture and the other half with the mozzarella and pea mixture. Press the two halves together and roll in the flour. Dredge in the beaten egg and then in breadcrumbs. Chill.

4 Heat the olive oil in a frying pan until hot. Add the *arancini* and sauté until they are golden brown on all sides. Drain on paper towels and allow to cool. Before serving, preheat the oven to 350°F. Place the croquettes on a baking sheet and bake for 5 minutes, until the crusts become crispy.

rice, pasta, gnocchi & polenta

shell pasta with cotechino sausage and lentils

conchiglie con cotechino e lenticchie

Another slant on the popular sausage-and-lentil theme. This is the sort of pasta dish that would be eaten as a main course during the New Year festivities. The best *cotechino* sausage requires a bit of work, but it is worth it (I can't really recommend the ready-cooked ones).

serves 4

1 x 18 oz *cotechino* sausage

3 tbsp olive oil

1 small onion, peeled and very finely sliced

¾ cup vegetable broth (see page 252), with a few saffron strands added

9 oz plum tomatoes, diced

2 fresh sage leaves, chopped

1 sprig fresh thyme

sea salt and freshly ground black pepper

¾ cup lentils (Castelluccio are best), cooked

a handful of fresh flat-leaf parsley, chopped

2 tbsp extra virgin olive oil

14 oz dried conchiglie pasta (shells)

freshly grated Parmesan to taste

1 Soak the *cotechino* sausage in warm water for 1 hour. Drain, pierce in several places with a fork and transfer to a saucepan with water to cook. Bring to a boil and simmer, covered, for 1½ hours. Leave in hot water until ready to use.

2 In a frying pan, heat the olive oil. Add the onion and half the broth, bring to a simmer, then cover and cook over low heat for 7-8 minutes. Add the tomatoes, raise the heat to high, and cook for another 3-4 minutes. Add the sage, half the thyme sprig, and salt and pepper to taste.

3 Remove the skin from the *cotechino* sausage and roughly chop the meat into small pieces. Add to the tomato sauce and cook for 10 minutes over medium heat. Add the cooked lentils, lower the heat and then simmer for a few minutes, adding the remaining vegetable broth if it becomes too thick. Season well with salt, pepper, parsley, the remaining thyme and extra virgin olive oil.

4 Meanwhile, cook the pasta in abundant boiling salted water until *al dente*. Drain well. Then add the pasta to the pan of lentils and toss over high heat for 30 seconds. Sprinkle with Parmesan and black pepper.

tagliatelle with fresh sausage sauce
tagliatelle con ragù di salsiccia

Sausages are a passion of the Italians. Don't feel limited to Italian sausages, though; buy any that are tasty. I once used some venison sausages from the local farmers' market.

serves 4-6

2 tbsp olive oil

1 x 28-oz can diced tomatoes

18 oz your favorite herb
   sausages, skinned and cut into
   1-inch lengths

1 celery stalk, diced

1 carrot, peeled and diced

1 small onion, peeled and chopped

½ tsp superfine granulated sugar

sea salt and freshly ground black
   pepper

14 oz tagliatelle

freshly grated pecorino to
   taste

1   Heat the olive oil and tomatoes together in a large saucepan. Add the sausage, celery, carrot, onion and sugar. Add enough water to just cover the ingredients and combine well. Season to taste and simmer for 45 minutes.

2   Cook the pasta in a large pan of boiling salted water until *al dente*.

3   Drain the pasta and transfer to a serving bowl. Add the sauce and toss well. Pass the grated cheese around for your guests to help themselves.

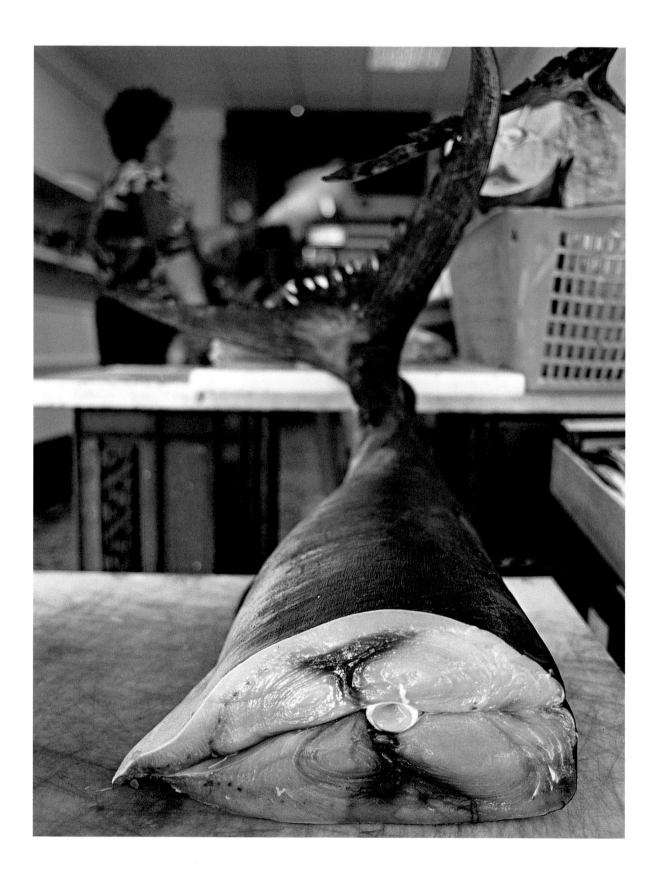

tagliatelle with swordfish and eggplant
pasta al pesce

Sicilians love swordfish and eggplant is equally highly prized in their cooking. This dish combines the two with the Italian classic, pasta.

serves 4

1 medium eggplant, cut into
  1-inch cubes
sea salt and freshly ground black
  pepper
4-5 tbsp olive oil
3 garlic cloves, peeled and thinly
  sliced
1 x 14.50-oz can diced tomatoes
18 oz swordfish steak, cut
  into ½-inch cubes
a small handful of flat-leaf
  parsley, finely chopped
a small handful of fresh marjoram,
  finely chopped
14 oz tagliatelle

1 Put the eggplant cubes into a colander, sprinkle with salt and leave to "degorge" for 20 minutes. Rinse and then dry thoroughly.

2 Heat half the olive oil in a pan, add the garlic and cook for 2 minutes, stirring. Add the tomatoes, season with salt and pepper and simmer for 10 minutes.

3 Meanwhile, heat the remaining olive oil and fry the eggplant in batches, adding more oil if necessary. Drain on paper towels and season with salt and pepper.

4 Add the eggplant, swordfish and most of the herbs to the tomato sauce and simmer slowly for a further 10 minutes.

5 Meanwhile, cook the tagliatelle in plenty of salted boiling water until *al dente*. Drain and mix with the swordfish sauce. Taste for seasoning. Garnish with the remaining herbs and serve immediately.

In Piedmont there are quite possibly more famous restaurants than in any other region of Italy. This is partly due to Piedmont's long association with France and French cuisine, but undoubtedly geography plays a part too. Piedmont's cooking is that of the colder north of Italy: there are plenty of dairy- and meat-oriented dishes with richer and more ornate saucing than is popular in the south.

Piedmont is a land of great variety of landscape, ranging from the encircling mountains of the north and west to the great plains of the valley of the Po. In the former, sheep and cattle produce milk for the famous Piedmontese cheeses – prime among them being fontina – while wheat, rice and other grains, as well as some superb fruit, are the produce of the latter.

Alba, home of the unique white truffle, is in Piedmont, and woods across the whole region are rich in the wild mushrooms for which the Italians have such a passion. Autumn is probably the time when Piedmontese *trattoria* food is at its best, and *Boccondivino* in Bra is a prime example of the region's fine *trattorias*.

osteria boccondivino

spaghetti with oven-roasted tomatoes, thyme and peppered pecorino

spaghetti con pomodori al forno, timo, e pecorino pepato

This is a simple but flavorful recipe, which can be prepared in several ways. The common denominator is fresh thyme, which helps blend the tomatoes with the peppery, spicy taste of the pecorino. In the winter I use oven-roasted tomatoes because they are more savory, but during summer try using fresh plum tomatoes if you can find them.

serves 4

1lb ripe plum tomatoes, halved

½ tbsp chopped fresh rosemary

3 tbsp chopped fresh thyme

1½ tsp superfine granulated sugar

3 garlic cloves, peeled

6 tbsp olive oil

a handful of fresh basil leaves

sea salt and freshly ground black pepper

14 oz spaghetti

3½ oz peppered pecorino, shaved (or regular pecorino plus freshly ground black pepper)

1 Preheat the oven to 300°F.

2 To make oven-roasted tomatoes, place the plum tomatoes on a baking sheet, cut sides up. Sprinkle with the rosemary, 1 tbsp of the thyme and the sugar. Chop 2 of the garlic cloves finely and sprinkle over the tomatoes with 4 tbsp of the oil. Bake for 2 hours. Allow the tomatoes to cool.

3 Heat the remaining olive oil in a frying pan. Add the remaining whole garlic clove and sauté until lightly golden – 1-2 minutes. Add the oven-roasted tomatoes and the basil and cook for 2-3 minutes over medium heat. Adjust the seasoning with salt and pepper to taste.

4 Cook the pasta in abundant boiling salted water until *al dente*. Drain well. Transfer the pasta to the tomatoes in the frying pan, then add the remaining thyme and the pecorino shavings. Toss and serve immediately.

farfalle carbonara with five vegetables
farfalle con carbonara di cinque verdure

"Carbonara" is a famous pasta dish seasoned with a sauce made with beaten egg and pancetta or bacon, and you will find it on many *trattoria* menus. It was originally created in honor of the American soldiers who liberated Italy: the combination of bacon, eggs and cream was meant to make them feel at home. This is my vegetarian version.

serves 4

9 oz broccoli florets

sea salt and freshly ground black
  pepper

4 tbsp olive oil

2 garlic cloves, peeled and
  chopped

2 zucchini, trimmed and diced

1 leek, white part only, washed
  and chopped

2 carrots, peeled and diced

1 red pepper, seeded and diced

a handful of fresh basil leaves,
  torn

2 large eggs, lightly beaten

1 cup Parmesan, freshly
  grated, plus extra to serve

14 oz farfalle pasta (bows)

1 Blanch the broccoli florets in boiling salted water for 2 minutes. Drain and set aside.

2 In a frying pan, heat the olive oil. Add the garlic and all the vegetables and sauté for 8 minutes. Season and add the basil.

3 In a bowl, combine the eggs with the Parmesan.

4 Meanwhile, cook the pasta in a large pan of boiling salted water until *al dente*. Drain well and transfer to a frying pan.

5 Toss the pasta with the vegetables over high heat for a few seconds. Turn down the heat. Stir in the egg-and-cheese mixture until well combined and "set," then season again. Serve immediately, with some extra freshly grated Parmesan if you like.

ATTENTI AL CANE

pasta with a tomato and vegetable sauce
bucatini alla marchigiana

The tremendous advantage of this simple sauce for pasta is that all its ingredients are available in winter. For this dish, local cooks would choose the greenest *verdicchio* or *vino cotto*, a syrup made by simmering grape juice over a gentle heat for several hours until it is thick.

serves 4-6

2 tbsp olive oil

1 small onion, peeled and finely
  chopped

1 celery stalk, chopped

1 carrot, peeled and chopped

3½ oz pancetta, diced

⅔ cup white wine

2 tbsp tomato paste

1lb ripe tomatoes, skinned
  and chopped, or canned tomatoes

leaves from 3 sprigs fresh thyme

leaves from 3 sprigs fresh
  marjoram

sea salt and freshly ground black
  pepper

1lb *bucatini* pasta

1 cup Parmesan cheese,
freshly grated

1 Heat the oil in a medium saucepan, then sauté the onion, celery and carrot for a few minutes.

2 Add the pancetta and mix. Add the wine and let it reduce until it has almost evaporated. Add the tomato paste, tomatoes, herbs and seasoning, bring to a boil, then turn down the heat and simmer, covered, for 20 minutes.

3 Meanwhile, cook the pasta in a large pan of boiling, salted water according to the instructions on the package. Drain and mix in a heated bowl with half the Parmesan and all the sauce. Pass around the remaining Parmesan for your guests to help themselves.

andrea's penne with arugula and tomato sauce

penne alla rucola e salsa di pomodori di Andrea

Penne is the ideal pasta shape of this dish, as the sauce clings to the pasta shape, making the dish deliciously substantial. This is one of my sister Andrea's favorite dishes.

serves 4-6

16 fresh tomatoes, skinned, seeded and diced

2 garlic cloves, peeled and finely chopped

2-3 tbsp olive oil

a handful of fresh basil, torn

sea salt and freshly ground black pepper

14 oz penne

16 arugula leaves, cut into strips

1⅛ cup Parmesan, freshly grated

1 Combine the tomatoes, garlic, oil and basil in a large bowl, then season and allow to rest.

2 Cook the pasta in rolling boiling salted water until *al dente*. Drain it, reserving ¾ cup of the water, and turn the pasta into the bowl with the tomato mixture. Toss well. Sprinkle the top with the arugula and Parmesan. Toss and taste for seasoning. Add a little pasta water if a thinner sauce is desired. Serve with extra freshly grated Parmesan if you like.

Seaside *trattorias* serve dishes like this – simple, everyday eating, with masses of flavor. I've published something similar before, but this is an upgrade, deleting the tomato and just allowing the clean flavors of the ingredients to sing out.

linguine with shrimp
linguine con gamberetti

serves 4–6

1 large onion, peeled

2 tbsp olive oil

1 garlic clove, peeled and chopped

a handful of fresh flat-leaf parsley, chopped

sea salt and freshly ground black pepper

18 oz jumbo shrimp, shelled and de-veined

14 oz linguine pasta (long flat strands)

1 Purée the onion in a food processor until creamy, or chop finely by hand. Put the onion, olive oil, garlic and 4 tbsp water into a large deep-sided frying pan. Cook over medium heat for 30 minutes until the water has almost evaporated, stirring often.

2 Add the parsley and some salt and pepper. Stir in the shrimp and simmer for 10 minutes.

3 Meanwhile, bring a large pan of salted water to a boil, and cook the linguine until *al dente*, stirring often. Drain the pasta and add to the onion and shrimp. Stir well and season again. Serve immediately.

ricotta gnocchi
tondore

This recipe is from my village, and has many variations and stories attached to it. It is served in virtually every *trattoria* along the Amalfi coast. My father loves this dish, and always laughs that everyone ends up with tomato sauce plastered on their clothes. He says it's a sign that you've eaten well.

serves 4

10½ oz ricotta cheese

⅔ cup all-purpose flour,
   plus extra for dusting

1 garlic clove, peeled and crushed

2 large egg yolks

sea salt and freshly ground black
   pepper

a little freshly grated nutmeg

to cook and serve

7 oz tasty cherry tomatoes,
   halved

2 tsp *peperoncino* (dried chili)

2 tbsp olive oil

a handful of fresh basil leaves,
   torn

Parmesan, grated, to taste

1 Mix all the *tondore* ingredients together in a bowl. Knead lightly on a floured surface. Roll into a sausage-shaped log the thickness of your little finger. Cut at an angle to create shapes the length of the first joint of your index finger.

2 Boil the gnocchi in batches in a large pan of boiling salted water. When they rise to the top of the pan, skim out into a frying pan.

3 Add the cherry tomatoes, *peperoncino* and olive oil to the frying pan, and sauté until the gnocchi are stained with tomato. Serve with torn basil and grated Parmesan.

baked potato dumplings

gnocchetti alla piemontese

Try to get a helper when making this dish, as it takes quite a bit of time; but it's worth it! The *gnocchetti* can be prepared hours in advance.

serves 4–6

1lb even-sized potatoes, scrubbed

¾ cup all-purpose flour

sea salt and freshly ground black pepper

7 oz fontina or Swiss cheese, thinly sliced

⅔ cup unsalted butter

1 Boil the potatoes in plenty of water. Drain and cool before peeling, then pass through a ricer or sieve; let the potato fall to the work surface like snow. Add the flour and 3 tsp salt and work the mixture into a dough with your hands.

2 Preheat the oven to 350°F. Break off small pieces of dough and roll them into sausage shapes, about 1 x ½-inch. Press each shape against the prongs of a fork, so the back is ridged and the front has an indentation. Place them well apart on a floured board.

3 Bring a large pan of salted water to a boil and poach the gnocchi, a few at a time, for 3 minutes. Put a layer of cooked gnocchi in a glass casserole dish, cover with slices of cheese, pats of butter and black pepper. Repeat until all ingredients are used, ending with cheese. Bake for 5 minutes.

pasta with pumpkin, sage and mozzarella
pasta con zucca, salvia, e mozzarella

This recipe comes from Renato Sozzani of *Albergo della Posta Ristorante Sozzani* in Sondrio, Lombardia. It is a very pretty building, in a romantic setting, and only has six tables! Family-run, the teenage children of the owners are the waiters. The marriage of sage, pumpkin and lemon is wonderful, and the mozzarella butter that slicks the pasta can be prepared well in advance.

serves 4

2 tbsp olive oil

18 oz pumpkin

sea salt and freshly ground black
   pepper

4 oz mozzarella, drained and
   finely diced

¼ cup unsalted butter,
   softened

2 garlic cloves, peeled and crushed

1 small handful fresh sage leaves,
   plus extra whole leaves to serve

juice and finely grated zest of
   1 unwaxed lemon

14 oz conchiglie pasta
   (shells)

¾ cup Parmesan, grated

1 Preheat the oven to 400°F.

2 Heat the olive oil in a roasting pan in the oven. Using a small sharp knife, peel the pumpkin, remove the seeds and cut the flesh into cubes of about ¾ inch. Add the pumpkin to the hot oil, season with salt and pepper and toss to coat. Roast for 30 minutes, turning from time to time, until tender and golden brown.

3 Put the mozzarella, butter, garlic, sage, lemon zest and juice and some salt and pepper in a food processor and blend to a coarse paste. Transfer to a sheet of parchment paper, roll into a cylinder, and chill until firm.

4 Meanwhile, bring a large saucepan of water to a boil. Add a good pinch of salt, then the pasta, and cook until *al dente*. Drain well.

5 Add the pumpkin to the pasta, then slice in the roll of cheese. Toss until the cheese has melted and coated the shells, then divide between four bowls, top with the reserved sage and serve sprinkled with Parmesan.

butternut squash, mozzarella and caramelized garlic risotto with shallots

risotto di zucca e mozzarella

This recipe comes from Geltrude Mitterman of *Trattoria Bella Vista* near Mendola, Alto Adige. It is family-run, very friendly, and very Austrian/Swiss in its interior and approach to its dishes.

serves 4

14 oz butternut squash
olive oil
1 small onion, peeled and diced
¼ cup unsalted butter
1 cup risotto rice
3 cups chicken broth
  (see page 253), hot
½ cup Parmesan, grated
4½ oz buffalo mozzarella,
  cut into ½-inch cubes
sea salt and freshly ground black
  pepper

pesto

1 large bunch fresh basil
3 garlic cloves, peeled
3 tbsp pine nuts, lightly toasted
about 3 tbsp olive oil
3 tbsp freshly grated Parmesan

1 First make the pesto. Put the basil, garlic and pine nuts in a food processor with a little salt and pepper. Work to a paste, then add enough olive oil to produce a loose-textured purée. Remove from the food processor, pour into a bowl and fold in the Parmesan.

2 Next, make the crispy shallots. Dust the shallots in seasoned flour, shake off any excess and deep-fry in vegetable oil at 320°F. When they are a light golden brown, remove from the oil using a slotted spoon and drain on a paper towel. Season with a little salt and keep ready on a warm plate.

3 To caramelize the garlic, first blanch the garlic in a pan of salted boiling water for about 3 minutes, then peel and transfer to a clean pan. Pour off the water and add the chicken broth and butter. Cook until the garlic is soft and the broth is reduced down to a syrup that coats the cloves.

4 Preheat the oven to 350°F.

5 Peel and seed the butternut squash, dice into ½-inch cubes and fry in a little olive oil until lightly colored. Transfer to the oven for 10-12 minutes, until the flesh is tender.

crispy shallots

2 oz shallots, peeled and
finely sliccd

¾ cup all purpose flour, seasoned

vegetable oil for deep-frying

caramelized garlic

16 garlic cloves

¾ cup chicken broth (see
page 253), hot

1¾ tbsp unsalted butter

6 Meanwhile, gently sweat the diced onion in the butter until the onion is soft. Add the rice to the onion, raise the heat and cook, stirring, until the rice is shiny and translucent. Lower the heat and begin to add the hot broth, a ladleful at a time. Stir into the rice and wait for it to be absorbed before you add the next ladleful.

7 Once the rice is cooked to *al dente*, and of the correct texture, fold in the Parmesan, mozzarella and squash, and cook for 2 minutes more. Season to taste.

8 Serve immediately on hot plates, drizzle the pesto around the risotto and top with a small pile of crisp shallots and caramelized garlic cloves.

rice, pasta, gnocchi & polenta

arugula sauce
sugo di rucola

This sauce is a smooth purée that combines arugula, walnuts and pine nuts – a sort of super-pesto. All over Italy, a version of it is used in huge quantities on pasta, *panini*, *bruschetta* and *foccaccini*, and it will happily spice up a risotto. This particular recipe comes from *Trattoria da Busse* in Venice, a charming and tiny place near St Mark's Square.

serves 6

6 oz arugula, trimmed and coarsely chopped

¼ cup shelled walnuts

⅓ cup pine nuts

1 small garlic clove, peeled

1¾ tbsp unsalted butter, softened

⅓ cup extra virgin olive oil

½ cup each of Parmesan and *Pecorino romano*, **freshly grated**

sea salt and freshly ground black pepper

1 Combine the arugula, walnuts, pine nuts and garlic in a food processor and process until the ingredients are finely chopped. Add the butter and oil and process until the mixture is creamy.

2 Transfer the mixture to a large bowl and stir in the cheeses. Season with salt and pepper to taste. Refrigerate the sauce until needed – it will keep for up to a week.

risotto with pancetta affumicata, buffalo mozzarella and savoy cabbage

risotto con pancetta, mozzarella e cavolo

I have based this recipe on one from Cinzia Cortosini, who owned *Vecchia Osteria del Ponte* at Bozzone, near Siena. They specialize in rice dishes, and this is a fine example. As a family, they originate from Milan, and they told me they wanted to stay true to their roots. Hence rice dishes form about half of their menu.

serves 4

4 oz *pancetta affumicata*, sliced

1 garlic clove, peeled and sliced

½-head Savoy cabbage, shredded into tiny pieces

sea salt and freshly ground black pepper

½ cup unsalted butter

1 medium onion, peeled and very finely chopped

2 cups risotto rice

⅔ cup dry white wine

6⅓ cups chicken broth (see page 253), hot

1½ cups Parmesan, grated

4½ oz buffalo mozzarella, drained and cut into small pieces

1 Cut the pancetta slices into matchsticks and fry them with the sliced garlic until golden. Toss in the shredded cabbage, place a lid on the pan and steam for about 5 minutes. Season, remove from the heat and set aside.

2 Melt the butter in a heavy-based saucepan. When it starts to foam add the chopped onion and cook on a reduced heat for 2-3 minutes, until soft but not brown.

3 Add the rice and stir continuously for about 3 minutes, until the rice becomes translucent. Pour in the wine and allow it to be absorbed. Start adding the simmering broth to the rice ladle by ladle, stirring continuously. The rice is cooked when it has a thick, creamy consistency, and an even *al dente* bite to it.

4 Incorporate the cooked pancetta and Savoy cabbage mixture into the rice, then fold in the Parmesan and mozzarella. Season well and serve immediately.

polenta, mozzarella and parma ham
panini con polenta, mozzarella e prosciutto

This recipe comes from *Trattoria Sorelle Carboni* in Recco, near Genoa. It serves simple, honest food, and this recipe is one of its specialities in the polenta season, from January to April. These small polenta "sandwiches" are ideal as an *antipasto*, or they could be served as an appetizer with drinks. Polenta is incredibly versatile, and this is one of the many ways – rather unusual – in which it can be used. Most people think of it as quite bland, but it can be exciting, as this and the following recipe demonstrate.

serves 6

3¼ cups water

1½ cups milk

sea salt and freshly ground black
  pepper

1¼ cups coarse polenta

⅓ cup unsalted butter

¾ cup Parmesan, grated, plus
  extra to serve

1 tbsp any mustard (optional)

12 oz buffalo mozzarella,
  sliced

7 oz Parma ham (*prosciutto
  di Parma*), thinly sliced

¾ cup all-purpose flour

2 large eggs, beaten

3¼ cups fresh breadcrumbs

vegetable oil for deep-frying

1 Bring the water, milk and a pinch of salt to a boil. Slowly whisk in the polenta and bring the mixture back to a boil, whisking constantly. Turn the heat down and leave the polenta to bubble, stirring as much as you can, for 35 minutes. At this stage the polenta should be coming away from the sides of the pan. Remove from the heat, add the butter, Parmesan and some pepper, then mix well.

2 Pour a thin layer of polenta into a lightly oiled tray and spread evenly. Allow to cool. Keep the rest of the polenta warm. When this first layer has cooled, spread a thin layer of mustard over it, if using, and arrange the mozzarella to cover the area. Lay the Parma ham over the mozzarella. Pour over the remaining warm polenta and spread it thinly to cover the filling. Cool the tray for at least 1 hour.

3 When cold, turn the entire tray out in one piece and cut into small neat triangles. Heat the oil for deep-frying. Coat each piece in flour, then the beaten egg, and finally coat with breadcrumbs. Deep-fry until crisp and golden brown.

grandmother furiani's radicchio lasagne

lasagne al radicchio della nonna Furioni

I once spent a fantastic weekend in Verona, staying with a family who grow and produce the best radicchio I have ever tasted. The grandmother of the family taught me how to cook and use radicchio in ways that I had never considered before.

serves 4

olive oil

1 onion, peeled and chopped

2 heads radicchio (red chicory),
   finely sliced

sea salt and freshly ground black
   pepper

10 sheets fresh, dried or
   oven-ready lasagne

white sauce

2¾ tbsp butter

3 tbsp all-purpose flour

1¼ cups milk

2¼ cups Parmesan or Gruyère,
   freshly grated

1 tsp freshly grated nutmeg

1 Preheat the oven to 375°F.

2 Heat a little oil in a frying pan, add the onion and fry until golden. Add the radicchio and fry for 4-6 minutes, until the radicchio has wilted. Add some salt and pepper to taste.

3 Cook the lasagne as directed on the package, if necessary (oven-ready needs no pre-cooking), then drain well.

4 To make the white sauce, melt the butter in a saucepan, add the flour and cook for 2-3 minutes, stirring. Remove the pan from the heat and gradually beat in the milk. Return to the heat and slowly bring to a boil, stirring all the time, until the sauce boils and thickens. Stir in three-quarters of the cheese, the radicchio mixture and the nutmeg.

5 Put a layer of sauce in the bottom of a square ovenproof dish. Place a layer of lasagne on top and then add another layer of sauce. Continue making layers, finishing with sauce. Cover the top with the remaining cheese.

6 Bake for 25 minutes, until golden. Serve immediately.

chicken livers and mushrooms with spaghetti

spaghetti con fegatini di pollo e funghi

This is a variation on a sauce said to have been created for the great singer, Caruso. Chicken livers are much loved in Italy, where they tend to use everything from the animal – an example of Italian frugality.

serves 4

14 oz dried spaghetti

sea salt and ground black pepper

1 tbsp extra virgin olive oil

¾ cup Parmesan, grated

tomato sauce

1 tbsp olive oil

1¾ tbsp unsalted butter

1 onion, peeled and finely diced

2 garlic cloves, peeled and crushed

12 small button mushrooms, halved

1 x 14.50-oz can diced tomatoes

1 tsp superfine granulated sugar

1¼ cups chicken broth (see page 253)

chicken liver sauce

1¾ tbsp unsalted butter

8 oz chicken livers, trimmed and sliced

1 tsp finely chopped fresh thyme

⅓ cup Marsala wine

finely chopped flat-leaf parsley

1 To make the tomato sauce, heat the oil and butter in a saucepan and cook the onion until soft. Add the garlic and mushrooms and cook for 2-3 minutes longer. Combine the tomatoes and sugar, add to the mushrooms, and cook over low heat for 10 minutes. Stir in the broth and simmer for 30 minutes, or until the sauce reduces and thickens. Season to taste with black pepper.

2 To make the chicken liver sauce, melt the butter in a saucepan, then add the chicken livers and thyme and cook over medium heat until brown. Increase the heat, stir in the Marsala and cook for 1-2 minutes. Stir in the parsley.

3 Cook the spaghetti in boiling salted water in a large saucepan until *al dente*. Drain and fold through the oil. Arrange half the spaghetti on a warm serving platter, top with half the chicken liver mixture, then half the tomato sauce and mix. Sprinkle over half the Parmesan, then repeat the layers. Mix together and serve immediately.

baked polenta with salami and tomatoes
polenta pasticciata

When polenta is presented as a pie and baked, it is known as "*polenta pasticciata*." There are many different versions – probably as many as there are homes in northern Italy – but this one is easy and is sure to draw compliments when served.

serves 4

4¼ cups water or
   vegetable broth (see page 252)

1⅓ cups coarse polenta

sea salt and freshly ground black
   pepper

⅓ cup butter

10½ oz mixed mushrooms
   (chestnuts, field, *porcini* or ceps),
   sliced

1 x 14.50-oz can Italian tomatoes,
   drained, seeds squeezed out and
   chopped

6 oz Italian salami, thinly
   sliced

½ cup Parmesan, grated

white sauce

2¾ tbsp butter

3 small bay leaves

3 tbsp all-purpose flour

2 cups milk

a pinch of freshly grated nutmeg

1 To make the white sauce, melt the butter in a small saucepan, add the bay, and stir in the flour. Cook over medium heat for 1 minute. Remove from the heat and gradually blend in the milk. Season with salt, pepper and nutmeg. Cook over medium heat, stirring constantly, until the sauce boils and thickens. Set aside, covered.

2 Place the water or broth in a large saucepan and bring to a boil. Gradually whisk in the polenta. Reduce the heat and cook for 20 minutes, stirring often. Season to taste.

3 Preheat the oven to 400°F. Melt half the butter in a frying pan and cook the mushrooms over low heat for 2-3 minutes. Season to taste with black pepper.

4 Remove the polenta from the heat and stir the remaining butter through. Spread one-third of the polenta into a greased ovenproof dish. Top with one-third of the mushrooms, one-third of the tomatoes, one-third of the salami and one-third of the white sauce. Repeat these layers twice, ending with a final layer of white sauce.

5 Sprinkle with Parmesan and bake for 30 minutes. Let stand for 5-10 minutes before serving.

fish & shellfish

baked stuffed tomatoes with shrimp
pomodori alla marsalese

This delicious, light dish is a Sicilian classic. *Trattorias* all over the island serve simple fish dishes such as this one.

serves 6

6 large, ripe firm tomatoes

1lb 10 oz cooked shrimp, shelled

2 oil-marinated anchovy fillets, finely chopped

a pinch of peperonico

9 oz pitted green olives, Sicilian if possible, chopped

3 tbsp olive oil

1 tbsp lemon juice

sea salt and freshly ground black pepper

a handful of fresh parsley

1 Preheat the oven to 400°F.

2 Cut about ¼-inch off the stem ends of each tomato. Keep this "lid." Remove the pulp and seeds from the insides of the tomatoes with a small spoon and discard.

3 In a large bowl, combine the shrimp, anchovies, peperonico and olives. Whisk together the olive oil and lemon juice and season to taste well with salt and pepper. Pour over the shrimp and toss well.

4 Spoon some of the shrimp mixture into the cavity of each tomato.

5 Put the tomatoes into a lightly oiled, shallow baking dish and bake for 15 minutes. Serve warm with a parsley sprig stuck in the top of each tomato.

lemon dressing
salmoriglio

This simple sauce/dressing – which is a marinade as well – tastes good with fish, especially swordfish steaks. It's also delicious with roast chicken or veal, and I really like it over artichoke or asparagus. It's handy to have in the refrigerator as it keeps for up to four days, and the longer it is left the more pungent it becomes.

serves 4

1 cup fruity extra virgin olive oil

juice of 2 lemons

a handful of fresh flat-leaf parsley, finely chopped

2 garlic cloves, peeled and chopped

1½ tsp dried oregano

sea salt and freshly ground black pepper

1 Off the heat combine ⅓ cup lukewarm water and half of the olive oil in a small saucepan. Whisk in the lemon juice, parsley, garlic and oregano and season to taste with salt and pepper.

2 Cook over a very, very low heat for 5 minutes, stirring often. Add the remaining oil.

OLSEN

CLAFOUTIS PESCHE
ed AMANEN
€ 11,90

The cooking of Piedmont has long been thought of as essentially French, for Turin – the region's major city – was the capital of the French province of Savoy, and French remained the court language until well into the 19th century. However, these days Turin is very much Italian, and it is a city of contrasts.

In the center of Turin there are countless *piazzas* and bridges over the Po. The encircling mountains are punctuated by a myriad of church spires and steeples. Yet on the outskirts it is relentlessly industrial.

The food of Turin is rich, creamy and quite French in feel. Chocolate is a local speciality – this is reputedly the first place in Europe to which it was introduced – as is the humble breadstick, or *grissini*. Pastries and desserts are a local passion too.

The *Cafe Olsen* – a simple, modern and youthful *torteria* in the middle of Turin – is one of the most perfect places I can think of in which to try a selection of Italian cakes and tarts.

cafe olsen

red mullet in paper

pesce al cartoccio

I love being served something wrapped in paper – there's such a sense of excitement and anticipation! The delicate flavor of the mullet here is enhanced by the savory strength of the anchovy butter. To make the envelopes for the fish you will need some parchment paper.

serves 4

4 red mullet, about 7 oz each

4 sprigs fennel fronds

a handful each of fresh basil and rosemary leaves

2 tbsp olive oil

sea salt and freshly ground black pepper

herb butter

⅔ cup unsalted butter

a handful each of fresh torn basil and chopped rosemary leaves

1 Preheat the oven to 425°F.

2 To make the herb butter, soften the butter and mash in the torn and chopped herbs. Chill until ready to use.

3 Wash, scale and gut the fish, leaving the livers in (your fishmonger will always do this for you). Dry the fish well, and put some of the fennel fronds and herbs in each cavity.

4 Cut the parchment paper into rectangles large enough to envelop each fish. Oil each fish and place in the center of the paper. Add another sprinkling of fennel and some salt and pepper, and close the paper parcels firmly.

5 Place the parcels on a baking tray and then bake for 12 minutes.

6 Serve the fish in their fragrant parcels, to be opened at the table, with the anchovy butter.

fennel and shrimp in a wine sauce

finocchio e gamberetti in salsa di vino

This is a wonderful way of serving jumbo shrimp: they are enhanced by the sweet aniseed flavor of fennel and set off by a simple wine sauce.

serves 4

1lb fennel bulbs (male and
  female – see page 61)

¾ cup dry white wine

1 onion, peeled and roughly
  chopped

1 garlic clove, peeled and halved

½ celery stalk, chopped

1 fresh bay leaf

sea salt and freshly ground black
  pepper

12 oz raw jumbo shrimp

4 tbsp extra virgin olive oil

a handful of fresh flat-leaf
  parsley, roughly chopped

1 Cut the fennel lengthways into quarters, and then into thin segments, being careful that each segment is attached to the central core – you want the segments to stay whole during the cooking. Wash and dry well.

2 Pour the wine into a frying pan and add the fennel, onion, garlic, celery, bay leaf, some salt and pepper and enough water to cover the fennel. Bring to a boil and cook uncovered until the fennel is tender but still *al dente*, about 7 minutes. Remove the fennel with a slotted spoon and put in a dish.

3 Throw the shrimp into the liquid and cook for 2 minutes. Fish them out with the slotted spoon and peel off the shells. Remove the veins, then place the shrimp in the dish with the fennel.

4 Now reduce the liquid by about half, then strain out and discard the vegetables. Mix the oil into the reduced wine, and pour over the shrimp and fennel. Scatter the parsley over the top.

squid sautéed with tomato and avocado
calamari saltati con pomodoro e avocado

Most *trattorias* on the coast would serve squid in some fashion, usually fairly plainly cooked. This must be an imported recipe because of the avocado, which is not grown in Italy.

serves 4

14 oz small squid, cleaned, prepared and sliced into ½-inch rings

sea salt and freshly ground black pepper

1 garlic clove, peeled and chopped

extra virgin olive oil

3 plum tomatoes, skinned, seeded and diced

1 avocado, peeled, pitted and diced

1 small red chili, seeded and chopped

a handful of fresh flat-leaf parsley, chopped

1 head radicchio (red chicory), separated into leaves

poaching liquid

5 cups cold water

1 tbsp white wine vinegar

1 carrot, peeled

1 onion, peeled

1 celery stalk

2 bay leaves

1 In a large pot, combine all the ingredients for the poaching liquid. Season with salt, cover the pot and bring to a boil. When the water is boiling, add the sliced squid and cook just until it turns white – 2-3 minutes. Drain well and set aside. Do not overcook the squid as it will become rubbery.

2 In a frying pan, sauté the garlic in 4 tbsp of the olive oil until fragrant – 1-2 minutes. Add the tomatoes, avocado and chili, and sauté for a few minutes just to heat through.

3 Add the squid rings and sauté for 1 minute, blending all the ingredients. Sprinkle with parsley and drizzle with extra virgin olive oil to taste. Season with salt and pepper and serve immediately on a bed of radicchio.

stewed cuttlefish with bitter greens in tomato sauce

totani in zimino

This Ligurian *trattoria* dish, which found its way to Tuscany, can be served with a side dish of steamed rice. It is said to be of Arab origin. The words *"in zimino"* come from the Arab word *"samin."* Through the centuries it has come to signify a method of cooking fish in butter or olive oil, and a sauce of green vegetables.

serves 4

18 oz cuttlefish or the
  smallest squid available

5 tbsp olive oil

2 garlic cloves, peeled and finely
  chopped

½ onion, peeled and chopped

1 celery stalk, finely minced

1 leek, washed and finely minced

sea salt and freshly ground black
  pepper

⅔ cup dry white wine

4-5 ripe plum tomatoes, quartered

1lb 10 oz Swiss chard or
  spinach

1 tsp chopped fresh chili

a handful of fresh flat-leaf parsley,
  chopped

1 Clean the cuttlefish, removing the black skin, eyes, mouth, ink sac and interior. Wash and rinse. Cut the tentacles into small pieces and the rest into strips ½-inch wide.

2 In a heavy-based frying pan heat 4 tbsp of the olive oil over medium heat. Add half the garlic and sauté until lightly golden. Add the onion, celery and leek and cook until tender but not brown – about 6-8 minutes. Add the cuttlefish, season with salt and pepper, and sauté for 3 minutes. Add the white wine and cook over medium-to-high heat until it evaporates. Add the tomato quarters and continue to cook over medium heat for 20 minutes. (If using squid, reduce this cooking time to about 5 minutes).

3 Meanwhile, wash and rinse the chard, then blanch in boiling water for 1 minute. Drain and chop coarsely. Place in a frying pan, cover and steam over high heat for 3-4 minutes, turning often. Wipe the pan, add the remaining olive oil and sauté the chard, remaining garlic and the chopped chili over medium heat for 5 minutes. Season. Stir the chard into the cuttlefish and continue to cook for a further 5 minutes. Sprinkle with the chopped parsley.

scallops with lemon, bay and rosemary oil

capasante con limone, alloro e olio di rosmarino

This recipe is so simple that it hardly needs a method. It's from the Naples area, where many of the best fish and shellfish recipes are to be found. The rosemary used here as a skewer grows in profusion all over Italy and it enhances fish dishes wonderfully.

serves 4

12 fat fresh scallops, coral removed
  (freeze and keep for stock)
4 tough rosemary stalks, leaves
  removed and retained
pared zest (cut into 12 pieces)
  and juice of 2 unwaxed lemons
12 fresh bay leaves
1½ tbsp olive oil
sea salt and freshly ground black
  pepper

1 Preheat the oven to 400°F.

2 Thread three scallops on to each rosemary stalk, alternating with three pieces of lemon zest and three bay leaves.

3 Pound the rosemary leaves and oil together until fine and pour over the scallops. Sprinkle with the lemon juice and leave to marinate for 20 minutes.

4 Season and bake in a roasting pan for 8 minutes only.

spicy scallops in mushrooms

capasante con funghi

Scallops, mushrooms and garlic are a wonderful combination in this quick dish, invented by my husband. He really knows how to cook all these ingredients and has taught me how to appreciate them. Serve with a little greenery such as arugula.

serves 4

¼ cup unsalted butter

18 oz button mushrooms (preferably organic), cleaned

4 shallots, peeled and finely chopped

2 garlic cloves, peeled and crushed

4 tbsp dry white wine

1 fresh red chili, seeded and finely sliced

a handful of fresh flat-leaf parsley, finely chopped

sea salt and freshly ground black pepper

12 large scallops, cleaned, and coral removed

1 Melt 2¾ tbsp of the butter in a large frying pan and cook the mushrooms, shallots and garlic for 4-5 minutes.

2 Stir the wine, chili and parsley into the mushroom mixture, and cook over high heat until the liquid has reduced by half. Taste for seasoning.

3 Meanwhile, heat the remaining butter in a frying pan and cook the scallops to seal, a couple of minutes only on each side.

4 Add the scallops to the sauce, and toss to combine.

trout wrapped in prosciutto
trote in fette di prosciutto

Trout in Italy is superb, and is served in *trattorias* in many different ways. This recipe comes from the *Trattoria Miranda* in Tellaro, near La Spezia, on the Ligurian coast. It is family-run and famous for its fish dishes. The recipe isn't difficult, and looks and tastes particularly good served at a dinner party.

serves 4

**4 medium trout, 9 oz each,
  scaled, gutted and cleaned**

1 tbsp olive oil

**8 long slices Parma ham
  (*prosciutto di Parma*)**

4 sprigs fresh thyme

marinade

5 tbsp olive oil

3 tbsp lemon juice

2 garlic cloves, peeled and crushed

1 tbsp chopped fresh thyme

**sea salt and freshly ground black
  pepper**

1 To make the marinade, combine the oil, lemon juice, garlic and thyme. Season to taste with black pepper and a touch of salt. Place the trout in a shallow dish, pour the marinade over, cover and refrigerate for 2 hours.

2 Preheat the oven to 350°F. Cut four pieces of parchment paper large enough to enclose each trout. Brush each sheet of paper with olive oil.

3 Place two slices of prosciutto side-by-side on each sheet of paper. Remove the trout from the marinade and place the prosciutto around the trout. Pour the remaining marinade over, and add a sprig of thyme to each fish. Fold the paper around the trout to enclose them. Seal the edges by rolling together tightly.

4 Place the parcels on an oven tray and bake for 20-25 minutes, or until the trout flesh flakes when tested. Serve immediately.

mussel, tomato and orange sauce

salsa di cozze, pomodori e arancia

Although called a sauce, which would be superb with pasta, this could also be served as a fish dish, a *"secondo piatto"* ("second course"). One would never imagine that mussels and oranges would go well together, but this Sicilian recipe, with its dash of chili, will surprise you.

serves 4

1½ tbsp olive oil

1 onion, peeled and chopped

1 garlic clove, peeled and chopped

½ tsp dried chili (*peperoncino*)

1 x 28-oz can diced tomatoes

¾ cup dry white wine

3 tsp finely chopped fresh
   oregano, or 1 tsp dried

½ tsp superfine granulated sugar

3 tbsp orange juice

freshly ground black pepper

16 mussels, cleaned and scrubbed

2 tsp finely grated orange zest
   from an unwaxed orange

a handful of fresh flat-leaf
   parsley, finely chopped

1 Heat the oil in a large saucepan and cook the onion, garlic and chili for 5 minutes. Mix in the tomatoes, half the wine, the oregano, sugar and orange juice. Season to taste with pepper. Bring to a boil, then reduce the heat and simmer for 40 minutes, or until the sauce reduces and thickens.

2 Preheat the oven to 400°F.

3 Place the mussels in a baking dish and pour in the remaining white wine. Bake for 8 minutes, or until the mussels open. Discard any unopened shells.

4 Combine the orange zest and parsley. Toss the mussels into the sauce, sprinkle with the parsley mixture and then serve.

sardine fritters with minted chili butter
frittelle di sardine con burro

Sardines are abundant in Italian waters, and the idea for the minted chili butter came from an old friend, Claudio Brugalossi, who runs *La Taverna* in Perugia. He spent 10 years in America and fulfilled a lifetime ambition to return to Italy with his wife and family to run his own *trattoria*. We used to teach together in Umbria; I did the vegetables and salads and he did the fish and meat. This recipe can be prepared several hours before cooking. Serve as an *antipasto*. Use the butter in tandem with many other small fish.

serves 4

12 fresh sardines, scaled

4 tbsp all-purpose flour

1 large egg, blended with 2 tbsp
  milk

1⅛ cup dried breadcrumbs

about 2 tbsp sunflower oil

minted chili butter

⅔ cup unsalted butter,
  softened

3 tbsp finely chopped fresh mint

2 spring onions or peeled shallots,
  finely chopped

1 garlic clove, peeled and crushed

1 small fresh red chili, seeded
  and finely chopped

freshly ground black pepper

1 Cut the heads from the sardines and, using scissors, cut along the underside of the fish. Clean, gut and open out flat. Cut the backbone at the tail end and remove. Separate the two fillets on each, so that you have 24 small pieces of fish. Wash the pieces and dry on some paper towel.

2 Coat the sardine pieces in flour, dip in the egg mixture, then coat with breadcrumbs. Cover and chill.

3 To make the minted chili butter, put the butter, mint, spring onions or shallots, garlic, chili and some pepper in a bowl and mix well. Place the butter on a piece of plastic wrap and roll into a log shape. Refrigerate.

4 Heat the oil and one-third of the minted chili butter in a large frying pan and cook the sardine fillets for 2 minutes on each side, or until golden.

5 Serve the sardines topped with a slice of the remaining minted chili butter.

seafood cannelloni with saffron sauce
cannelloni con frutta di mare

The *Serra Gambetta* in Apulia is run by Signora Perna Lanera and her son Domenico. Their *agritorismo* is on the coast, and surrounded by olive groves, vineyards, wheat fields and almond trees. They love seafood, and although this recipe – one of their classics – appears time-consuming, it's very easy.

serves 4

8 lasagne sheets, blanched

filling

1¾ tbsp butter

10½ oz firm-fleshed white
  fish fillets, cut in bite-sized pieces

8 medium scallops, shelled and cut
  in bite-sized pieces

sea salt and freshly ground black
  pepper

juice of 1 unwaxed lemon

10½ oz ricotta, drained

1 large egg, lightly beaten

1 tsp finely chopped flat-leaf parsley

2 tsp snipped fresh chives

freshly ground nutmeg

saffron sauce

1¾ tbsp butter

2 shallots, peeled and finely chopped

1 garlic clove, peeled and crushed

a pinch of pure saffron powder

1¼ cups table cream

1 Preheat the oven to 350°F.

2 To make the filling, melt the butter in a saucepan and cook the fish and scallops for 2-3 minutes on each side, or until just opaque. Season to taste with pepper and lemon juice. Transfer to a bowl using a slotted spoon. Pour off the pan juices and reserve.

3 Add the ricotta, egg, parsley and chives to the bowl, and season to taste with nutmeg. Mix to combine.

4 To make the sauce, melt the butter in a pan and cook the shallot and garlic for 4-5 minutes. Add saffron to taste and cook for 1 more minute, then pour in the cream and reserved seafood juices and season to taste with salt and pepper. Bring to a boil, reduce the heat and simmer, stirring occasionally, for 5 minutes, or until the sauce thickens slightly. Strain and discard any solids.

5 To make the cannelloni, place some filling down the center of each pasta sheet. Roll up to form a thick tube. Arrange the cannelloni in a greased ovenproof dish. Pour the sauce over and cover with foil. Bake for 20 minutes, or until thoroughly heated through. Serve immediately.

meat & poultry

pork tenderloin baked in pastry

filetto di maiale e prosciutto in crosta

This is a recipe for a special occasion, whether you're cooking at home or eating in a *trattoria*. It is the Italian version – a poor man's version perhaps – of Beef Wellington, but it looks very stylish and is perfect for entertaining, as it can be prepared in advance and kept in the wings, ready to go. It would be great for a wedding meal, for instance.

serves 6

1lb pork tenderloin

sea salt and freshly ground black pepper

2-3 tsp chopped fresh rosemary

10 slices Parma ham (*prosciutto di Parma*)

1 large egg, beaten, for glaze

pastry

1½ cups all-purpose flour

a pinch of salt

1¼ tbsp unsalted butter, diced

approx. 2 tbsp ice-cold water to bind

1 Preheat the oven to 375°F.

2 First make the pastry. Mix the flour and salt together, then rub in the butter until it resembles breadcrumbs. Add enough water to bind into a damp ball. Wrap in plastic wrap and refrigerate for 20 minutes.

3 Lightly season the pork tenderloin, being more generous with pepper than salt, and sprinkle with the rosemary. Wrap the pork in the ham slices, overlapping them. Put it on a baking sheet.

4 Roll the pastry out to the length of the pork and drape the pastry over the pork, tucking it in under the meat. It doesn't need to be completely sealed.

5 Brush with beaten egg and bake for 40 minutes, until the pastry is golden.

6 Allow the meat to relax for about 15 minutes before slicing. Serve without a sauce.

veal with a mushroom cream sauce
vitello alla crema di funghi

This classic veal recipe is based on a recipe from *Cibrèo*, a *ristorante par excellence* in Florence. It uses veal and the seasonal mushrooms that appear from late September onward. This would be the "dish of the day" at that time, without a shadow of a doubt.

serves 6

1 celery stalk, trimmed and
  chopped
1 carrot, peeled and chopped
2 whole cloves
3 bay leaves (fresh are stronger)
½ cup dry vermouth or
  white wine
12 shallots, peeled
18 oz field mushrooms,
  cleaned and chopped
1¼ cups chicken broth (see
  page 253)
2 large egg yolks
4 tbsp whipping cream
sea salt and freshly ground black
  pepper
6 veal escalopes, cut about
  ¼-inch thick
2 tbsp all-purpose flour
3 tbsp olive oil
chopped fresh flat-leaf parsley for
  garnish (optional)

1 Put the celery, carrot, cloves and bay leaves on a square of muslin and tie into a bag with string. Place this in a heavy-based saucepan with the vermouth or wine, bring to a boil and reduce the liquid by about half.

2 Add the shallots, mushrooms and broth, bring back to a boil and cover and simmer for 30 minutes. Discard the muslin bag.

3 Whisk together the egg yolks and cream, then whisk in a little of the hot cooking juices. Slowly pour the egg yolk and cream mixture into the saucepan, stirring rapidly to prevent lumps forming. Season to taste. Reduce the heat to very low. Cook gently, stirring constantly, until the sauce has thickened. Do not allow to boil. Keep warm.

4 Beat the escalopes to tenderize them a little. Sprinkle with 1 level tsp salt and ½ level tsp pepper. Coat lightly with flour.

5 Heat a third of the olive oil in a frying pan, and lightly brown the escalopes two at a time for 3 minutes on each side, or until cooked. Remove from the pan and serve the sauce over the top. Garnish with parsley if desired.

la dimora dei cavalieri

Basilicata, also known by its Latin name of *Lucania*, is said to be the poorest region of Italy. It lies on the instep of the Italian boot, and is hot, dry and mountainous, with only a short coastline.

The pig rules in Basilicata, and when the family animal is killed in the autumn, nothing is wasted. *Lucaneca* is the most famous sausage (called *luganega* in the north). Chili is the predominant flavoring in the region, and sauces for the many unique, home-made pasta shapes are packed with fieriness.

The *Azienda Agristico La Dimora dei Cavaliere* in Vaglio is an unusual *trattoria*. A businessman from the north is its owner, but the *azienda* is his baby, and specializes in the Lucano cuisine.

Very modern, *La Dimora dei Cavaliere* is set on top of a hill, with beautiful views to every side. The food is simple, very good value, with fresh pasta made on site daily, and wines made locally by a relative. It also has rooms, so you can stay and be charmed for even longer.

sausages with lentils

lenticchie con salsiccia piccante

This is a perfect New Year's Eve dish, as lentils are believed to bring money when eaten at the beginning of the year. *Mostarda di Cremona*, a candied fruit chutney in mustard syrup, is available in Italian shops.

serves 6

1½ cups dried green Italian small lentils (those from Castelluccio are best)

2 tbsp olive oil

1 onion, peeled and chopped

1 carrot, peeled and diced

1 celery stalk, chopped

9 oz diced pancetta

1¼ cups beef broth (see page 254)

1 bouquet garni (2 bay leaves, 2 sprigs rosemary, 3 sprigs thyme, 3 sprigs parsley)

6 fresh Italian sweet sausages

sea salt and freshly ground black pepper

6 tbsp *mostarda di Cremona* or other mixed fruit chutney with mustard seeds, coarsely chopped

1 Soak the lentils for 30 minutes in water to cover.

2 Heat the olive oil in a large frying pan, and sauté the onion over medium heat until lightly golden. Add the carrot, celery and pancetta and cook for a few minutes until golden brown.

3 Drain the lentils, add to the pan and sauté for 2 minutes. Add 1 cup of the beef broth and the bouquet garni, cover and bring to a boil. Lower the heat and simmer for 1½ hours. Do keep an eye on the liquid, adding more broth if necessary.

4 Heat a grill pan. Butterfly the sausages by slicing them lengthways, but not quite through, and grill on both sides until browned, crisp and cooked.

5 Season the lentils and serve with the grilled sausages and 1 tbsp of candied fruit chutney in its syrup.

filled lamb rolls
bracioline

This is a variation of one of my grandmother's recipes – and is a great example of how meat is served in Italy, either in the *trattoria* or home. The meat is prepared simply and should be of the finest quality.

serves 6

2lb top round of leg of
lamb, cut into ⅛inch thick slices

3 tbsp olive oil, plus extra for oiling

sea salt and freshly ground black
  pepper

18 bay leaves (fresh are best)

2 onions, peeled and cut into 18
  small wedges

a handful of fine breadcrumbs

filling

4 tbsp olive oil

1 onion, peeled and finely chopped

3½ oz pecorino cheese,
cubed

3½ oz pancetta cubed

1½ cups bread, cubed

a handful of fresh flat-leaf
  parsley, chopped

1 large egg, beaten

1 To make the filling, heat the olive oil in a saucepan, then sauté the onion until golden – 5-8 minutes. Remove from the heat and allow to cool. Add the pecorino, pancetta, bread, parsley and egg and mix well. Season to taste with salt and black pepper.

2 Beat the meat slices to tenderize them. Cut the slices into 3-inch squares. Put 1 scant tbsp of filling on each slice of meat, near a corner. Roll the corner of meat over the stuffing, tuck in the edges and roll it into a small sausage shape, about 1½ inches thick x 3 inches long. Continue until all the meat rolls are done.

3 Preheat the oven to 400°F.

4 Oil a baking sheet and sprinkle it with salt. Push two skewers through the side of a meat roll; add a bay leaf and a wedge of onion. Repeat, alternating the meat, bay and onion, to fill each double-skewer with 3 meat rolls.

5 Pour 3 tbsp olive oil on to a flat plate and put the breadcrumbs on a second plate. Dip each skewer in the oil, then in the breadcrumbs. Arrange in a roasting pan and roast for 20 minutes, turning after 10 minutes.

fricassée of artichoke and lamb

fricassea di agnello e carciofi

This really delicious lamb recipe is best served with cooked and cooled green beans dressed like a salad with oil, vinegar, salt and pepper.

serves 6

juice of 2 lemons

2 globe artichokes, tough leaves removed

2lb boneless leg of lamb

4 tbsp olive oil

2 tbsp fresh flat-leaf parsley, chopped

3 garlic cloves, peeled and thinly sliced

⅔ cup dry white wine

sea salt and freshly ground black pepper

1 medium egg yolk

1 Pour the juice of 1 lemon into a bowl of cold water. Peel one artichoke stem, then cut the top off the artichoke leaves – approximately ¼ inch from the top. Start peeling the leaves off the artichoke – at least four layers – until a pale yellow is revealed. Put into the acidulated water and repeat with the other artichoke. Cut the artichokes into quarters and remove the fuzzy chokes and prickly purple leaves at the base. Return the quarters to the acidulated water. Peel off any remaining outside part of the stalks, leaving only the tender marrow. Cut this into rounds and throw into the acidulated water.

2 To prepare the lamb, remove the fat and gristle from the outside of the leg and any nuggets of fat lurking on the inside. Cut the meat into 1-inch chunks.

3 Preheat the oven to 300°F. Heat the oil in a casserole dish. Add the herbs and garlic and sauté. Add the lamb and then the wine and boil for 1 minute.

4 Drain the artichoke pieces and add to the casserole dish. Season. Cover and bake for 1 hour, or until the meat is cooked through and tender, adding a little hot water if the liquid runs dry. Towards the end of the cooking time, beat together the egg yolk and juice of 1 lemon, pour over the meat and stir well. Check the seasoning and serve.

pork, sausage and prosciutto skewers
spiedini di maiale, salcicce e prosciutto

This recipe makes me think of starving Tuscan hunters, coming into the *trattoria* after an early morning start, to eat a late breakfast. In fact it would make an ideal brunch recipe here – it's flavorful, filling and quick.

serves 4

4 generous herby sausages

2 pork filet steaks

12 fresh bay leaves

3 lemons, each cut into 4 wedges

12 slices Parma ham (*prosciutto di Parma*)

3-inch square thick slices of coarse-textured bread

a handful each of fresh sage and thyme leaves, chopped

sea salt and freshly ground black pepper

1 Preheat the oven to 400°F, and have ready four long skewers.

2 Cut each sausage into three equal pieces, and each steak into 6 equal pieces.

3 Arrange all the ingredients on the skewers evenly: first the sausage, then the bay leaf, pork, lemon, prosciutto and bread. Repeat until the ingredients are divided equally between the four skewers.

4 Sprinkle with the herbs and salt and pepper, and bake for 10-12 minutes, or until thoroughly cooked. Serve at once.

spatchcock chicken with ricotta and herbs

pollo piccolo alla ricotta ed erbe

The simple chicken dish will impress guests, whether in a *trattoria* or in the home, and has the advantage of being simple to prepare.

serves 4

4 x 1lb organic, free-range
  spatchcock chickens, prepared,
  cleaned and dried

2 tbsp olive oil

4 fresh rosemary sprigs

freshly ground black pepper

1½ cups dry white wine

stuffing

5½ oz ricotta

2 oz fontina cheese, finely
  grated

2 oz Gorgonzola cheese,
  crumbled

4 slices mortadella, finely
  chopped (optional)

a handful of fresh flat-leaf parsley

1 tbsp chopped fresh marjoram

1 tbsp chopped fresh sage

1¾ tbsp butter, melted

1 Preheat the oven to 425°F.

2 To make the stuffing, place the ricotta, fontina, Gorgonzola, mortadella, parsley, marjoram, sage and butter in a bowl and mix. Divide into four portions.

3 Gently ease the skin from the chicken breast of each bird and spoon the stuffing into the pocket. Brush each bird with olive oil and top with a sprig of rosemary and a sprinkle of black pepper.

4 Place the birds on a roasting rack in a baking dish then pour over the wine. Roast for 25-30 minutes, depending on the size. Reduce the heat to 350°F and cook for a further 15 minutes, until the chicken is cooked through, basting with the pan juices often.

5 Remove the birds and set aside to keep warm. Place the baking dish over a hot plate and bring the juices to a boil, then pour over the birds and serve.

chicken marsala

pollo al marsala

Many *trattorias* or families would serve something like this for Sunday lunch. It is very family-friendly.

serves 4

**4 medium organic free-range
  chicken breast filets, pounded**

seasoned all-purpose flour

1¾ tbsp unsalted butter

2 tbsp olive oil

¾ cup dry Marsala

4 tbsp chicken stock

1¾ tbsp butter, softened

**sea salt and freshly ground black
  pepper**

1 Coat the chicken in flour and shake off the excess. Heat the butter and oil together in a frying pan until the butter is foaming. Add the chicken and cook for 3 minutes on each side.

2 Stir in the Marsala and bring to a boil. Cover and simmer for 25-30 minutes, or until the chicken is cooked through, turning the meat occasionally.

3 Remove the chicken and set aside to keep warm. Add the stock to the Marsala and bring it to a boil. Boil for 2 minutes. Whisk in the softened butter and season to taste with black pepper.

4 To serve, spoon the sauce over the chicken.

veal flat steaks
polpettone di vitello

For my sister Gina, who just loves this home-made dish, which changes quite frequently according to whatever takes my fancy.

serves 6

1lb minced veal

1 garlic clove, peeled and crushed

a handful of fresh flat-leaf parsley, finely chopped

sea salt and freshly ground black pepper

1 tbsp tomato paste

1 large egg, beaten

4 medium slices of bread (crusts removed)

$\frac{1}{3}$ cup white wine

a handful of fresh breadcrumbs

2 tbsp olive oil

1 Combine the veal, garlic, parsley, salt and pepper to taste, tomato paste and egg.

2 Put the bread in a bowl and pour over the wine. Leave for a few minutes, until the bread has softened. Remove the bread and add it to the meat mixture, then beat well with a wooden spoon.

3 Shape the mixture into six flat steaks, then dip them in breadcrumbs. Heat the olive oil in a large frying pan and, when it is hot, brown the steaks on both sides. Cover the frying pan with a lid and cook for 7 minutes, or until the meat is cooked. Serve.

bolognese veal cutlets

cotolette alla bolognese

Veal is hugely popular in Italy, in *trattorias*, restaurants, and in the home, particularly in the south.

serves 4

1 medium egg

sea salt and freshly ground black
  pepper

8 tbsp fine white breadcrumbs

4 veal cutlets, about 4½ oz each

¼ cup unsalted butter

1 tbsp olive oil

2 oz Parma ham (*prosciutto di
Parma*), thinly sliced

2 oz Parmesan cheese, cut
  into shavings

tomato sauce

1 tbsp butter

1 tbsp very finely chopped onion

6 tbsp tomato sauce

4 tbsp meat or vegetable stock

1 For the sauce, heat the butter in a pan, then add the onion and a pinch of salt and sauté for 5 minutes. Add the tomato sauce and cook for 10 minutes. Add the stock, cover, bring to a boil and simmer for 5 minutes. Season.

2 In a bowl, beat the egg with 1 tsp of salt. Spread the breadcrumbs on a plate. Coat the veal on both sides in the egg, then in the crumbs, pressing them on to form a thick layer. Chill, covered. In a frying pan big enough to hold the steaks one next to the other, heat the butter and oil until the foam subsides. Fry the cutlets until golden, turn and repeat.

3 Put a quarter of the *prosciutto* on each steak, and put a quarter of the Parmesan on each *prosciutto*. Spoon the sauce over the meat. Cover with a lid and cook over low heat for 7-10 minutes, or until the meat is cooked. Serve.

veal noisettes in mushrooms and garlic
noisette di vitello ai funghi porcini

This is a Venetian classic. In Venice they use fresh *porcini* during the short period when they're in season, from the end of September to early October. However, I use field mushrooms as they have tons of flavor and are easy to find.

serves 4

2 tbsp olive oil

9 oz field mushrooms, sliced

2 garlic cloves, peeled and finely chopped

a handful of fresh flat-leaf parsley, chopped

a little all-purpose flour, for dusting

8 veal noisettes, about 2 oz each

¼ cup unsalted butter

sea salt and freshly ground black pepper

4 tbsp dry white wine

1 Heat half the olive oil in a large frying pan and cook the mushrooms, garlic and parsley until tender. Set aside.

2 Lightly flour the veal noisettes. Using a large frying pan, heat the remaining oil with the butter. Add the noisettes and cook for 5 minutes on each side. Season, remove from the pan and keep warm. Pour the wine into the pan and let it reduce slightly, then add the mushrooms.

3 Arrange the veal on a serving dish and pour over the mushrooms and garlic.

PE(CHE

Miele
Italiano
Carboni Mire Fiori
......sa, Rigutino, 45 - Tel. 0575/978860
peso netto gr. 1000

veal and pork meatballs

polpette alla ferrigno

Meatballs are a family dish and are slightly celebratory in feel – because they take quite a time to make. You will occasionally find them on a *trattoria* menu. You must use the best possible meat, and get the butcher to mince it as finely as he can for that melt-in-your-mouth effect. Never use ordinary butcher's mince, as it is too coarse and fatty, and meatballs made with it will fall apart.

serves 8

18 oz minced veal

18 oz minced pork

2 large eggs

a handful of fresh flat-leaf parsley, chopped

1¼ cups Parmesan, grated

2 slices stale bread, soaked in milk and squeezed dry

4½ oz diced pancetta

sea salt and freshly ground black pepper

to cook

2-3 tbsp olive oil

1 medium onion, peeled and finely chopped

2-3 tbsp tomato paste

½ tsp superfine granulated sugar

1 Mix all the meatball ingredients together in a large bowl. Shape into about 24 even-sized balls. Using your hands is the easiest method. Flatten slightly into oval shapes about ½-inch thick.

2 Heat the olive oil in a large frying pan and fry the balls until well browned on each side. Transfer to a casserole dish.

3 Add the onion, tomato paste, sugar and ¾ cup water to the frying pan, stirring. Cook for 5-10 minutes, then season with salt and pepper.

4 Pour the sauce over the meatballs, adding enough water to almost cover them. Cover and simmer over low heat for 1 hour.

veal and cheese skewers
spiedini di vitello e formaggio

We Italians love food on skewers – it brings out the fighting spirit in our blood. *Trattorias* specialize in food like this – dishes that are simple to prepare and yet really impressive. But this dish is also great for the busy home cook because it takes so little time to prepare. The better the quality of the veal, the tastier the dish will be. I often mince my own veal to make sure it's very fine.

serves 4

1lb minced veal

8 green olives, pitted and finely chopped

2 small garlic cloves, peeled and finely chopped

zest of 2 lemons (unwaxed are best)

3 tbsp olive oil

a handful of fresh flat-leaf parsley, chopped

sea salt and freshly ground black pepper

3 oz *bocconcini* mozzarella or ordinary mozzarella

24 vine-ripened cherry tomatoes

24 basil leaves

1 In a bowl, combine the veal, olives, garlic, lemon zest, 1 tbsp olive oil, parsley, and salt and pepper to taste.

2 Divide the mixture into 24 even balls, about 1 inch in diameter each, and cut the *bocconcini* or mozzarella into 24 pieces.

3 Take one portion of the veal mixture and flatten it out in the palm of your hand. Place a piece of cheese inside, then wrap and roll it to form an even-shaped ball. Repeat to make all the balls.

4 Using a heavy-based frying pan, heat the remaining olive oil. Fry the balls in batches for 5 minutes, or until cooked, ensuring they are evenly fried on all sides, then remove from the heat to a paper towel. Return the pan to the heat and flash-fry the tomatoes.

5 Put a veal ball onto a skewer, then a basil leaf, then a tomato, until you have six of each ingredient on each skewer. Serve immediately.

chunky meat sauce with vegetables
sugo di carne alla fiammetta

Fiammetta ran the *Trattoria di Montagliari* in Chianti, and this is her husband's favorite recipe. It's called a *sugo*, or sauce, but in reality it is more like a meat stew, to be served with potatoes and vegetables, although it would be delicious with pasta too.

serves 8

2 medium onions, peeled

1 medium carrot, peeled

1½ celery stalks

4 tbsp olive oil

1¾ tbsp unsalted butter

5 sprigs fresh flat-leaf parsley,
chopped

1lb boneless beef sirloin

12 oz boneless pork shoulder

8 oz sweet Italian sausage,
without fennel seeds, casing
removed

sea salt and freshly ground black
pepper

1 cup dry red wine, preferably
Chianti

1 tbsp tomato paste

2-3¼ cups beef broth
(see page 254)

1 Dice the onions, carrot and celery into ½-inch pieces.
Heat the olive oil and butter together in a large heavy-
based flameproof casserole dish over medium-to-low
heat. Add the vegetables and parsley and cook slowly,
tossing occasionally, until very tender – about 20 minutes.

2 Dice the beef, pork and sausage into ½-inch pieces. Add
the meat to the casserole dish and increase the heat to
medium. Cook, tossing frequently, just until the meat has
lost its raw colour. Season well with salt and pepper to
taste. Pour in the red wine and simmer briskly until the
wine has reduced by half.

3 In a small bowl blend the tomato paste with 1½ tbsp of
the broth. Stir this mixture into the casserole dish and
add an additional ½ cup of broth. Simmer the sauce,
covered, for 1½ hours, or until the meat is cooked
through, adding broth ½ cup at a time to keep the sauce
from becoming too thick and sticking to the bottom. It
may not be necessary to use all the broth. Taste the sauce
and season again if necessary.

grilled beef on a skewer
tzigonie

Mario Gianni owns *Trattoria Baffo* in the Valtellina region of Piedmont, and his grilled beef on a skewer is an Alpine dish seldom seen today. The beef is slightly fiddly to cut, but you could get the butcher to do it for you. The end result is well worth while, as it looks really impressive. He serves it with fried or roasted potatoes and tossed garden salad. You will need 10 to 12 wooden skewers 9 inches long.

serves 5-6

olive oil

12 oz boneless beef sirloin,
 very thinly sliced, about $\frac{1}{8}$-inch
thick, about 10-12

2 tsp fresh rosemary leaves,
 chopped

sea salt and freshly ground black
 pepper

1 Preheat a ridged cast-iron stove-top grill or a broiler. Rub the skewers with olive oil and allow it to soak into the wood. Do this three or four times before grilling.

2 Wrap the slices of beef tightly around the sticks, leaving 2-3 inches of wood exposed at each end of the skewer. Secure with a wooden toothpick if necessary. Cover the exposed ends of the skewers with foil.

3 Rub the beef with olive oil and sprinkle with chopped rosemary. Place the skewers on or under the hot grill. Brown lightly on all sides, until cooked to your taste, and sprinkle with salt and pepper to taste.

veal cutlets stuffed with mozzarella
cotolette di vitello con mozzarella

This recipe is inspired by Dino Boscorato of the *Trattoria dall'Amelia* in Mestre, a charming *trattoria* in the side streets near the canal. It serves very traditional dishes, and offers wonderful hospitality. When I had this dish there, they sautéed the salad leaves rather than serving them fresh.

serves 4

4 veal cutlets, about 7 oz
  each
sea salt and freshly ground black
  pepper
½ cup olive oil
5½ oz fresh porcini (ceps) or
  wild mushrooms, cleaned and
  sliced
1 garlic clove, peeled and sliced
2 tbsp chopped fresh flat-leaf
  parsley
8 oz buffalo mozzarella,
  diced
2 tomatoes, skinned and diced
1⅛ cup Parmesan, grated
¼ cup butter
a few sprigs fresh rosemary
8 oz mixed salad leaves
  (endive, radicchio lettuce and
  arugula)
24 basil leaves

1 Preheat the oven to 375°F.

2 Slice the veal cutlets in half lengthways and flatten each half slightly. Season with salt and pepper.

3 Heat half the olive oil and sauté the mushrooms with the garlic and parsley until the garlic is golden.

4 Divide the mozzarella between four veal cutlet halves, along with a few pieces of tomato, some grated Parmesan and half the fried mushrooms (the rest are for the sauce). Place the other veal cutlet halves on top, sealing the edges by pressing down with the back of a knife blade.

5 Heat the remaining olive oil with most of the butter in a frying pan, add the rosemary and some salt and pepper, and sauté the cutlets until they are golden brown. Then cook in the oven for 8-9 minutes.

6 Meanwhile, place the remaining fried mushrooms in the frying pan with the veal juices still in it. Add the remaining butter and simmer for a few minutes. Season well. Arrange a bed of salad leaves on four serving plates. Place the veal in the middle and spoon over the sauce.

braised veal rolls
rollatine di vitello

This recipe comes from the *Agriturismo La Viranda*, in the Monferrato zone of Piedmont west of Turin, which has been in existence for more than ten years. Veal, the most popular meat in Italy, is often made into rolls – showing the Italian love of "parcels" again – and this classic dish is substantial and delicious.

serves 6

1½lb boned loin of veal

2 oz Parma ham (*prosciutto di Parma*), coarsely chopped

1 small onion, peeled and coarsely chopped

2 small garlic cloves, peeled and coarsely chopped

2 tbsp coarsely chopped fresh flat-leaf parsley leaves

½ tsp chopped fresh rosemary leaves, plus 1 sprig

3 tbsp olive oil

4 large canned plum tomatoes, drained and finely chopped

½ cup dry white wine

⅔ cup beef broth (see page 254)

8 small sage leaves

sea salt and freshly ground black pepper

1 Get the butcher to cut the veal into thin slices – about 12 *scaloppini*, then at home pound them lightly to make them slightly larger and thinner and to tenderize the fibres. Combine the *prosciutto*, onion, garlic, parsley and chopped rosemary on a cutting board. Chop until very fine. Arrange the *scaloppini* on a work surface and spoon equal amounts of filling on to the center of each. Roll up, tucking in the sides to enclose the filling. Tie with thin string.

2 Heat the olive oil in a medium-heavy sauté pan over medium-to-high heat. Add six meat rolls and brown them evenly on all sides. Transfer them to a small platter. Brown the remaining rolls and add these to the platter. Add the tomatoes to the pan and simmer briskly for 2 minutes. Pour in the wine and simmer for 2 minutes. Return the meat rolls to the pan and pour the broth over them. Add the rosemary sprig and sage and season.

3 Gently simmer the meat rolls, partially covered, stirring occasionally, for 35 minutes, or until tender. Transfer the meat rolls to a shallow serving platter and snip off the string. Simmer the sauce to thicken it slightly. Discard the rosemary, spoon the sauce over the meat rolls, and serve.

braised shin of veal

ossobuco alla milanese

"Ossobuco" means "marrow bones," and this dish is a speciality of Milan. This particular recipe comes from Antonio Stoppani of Peck in Milan. Peck is the most famous food store in Italy, and they have a café in the next road, where *ossobuco* is often to be found on the menu. In Italy this dish is almost the equivalent of shepherd's pie.

serves 4

1¾ tbsp unsalted butter

1 carrot, peeled and chopped

2 onions, peeled and chopped

2 celery stalks, chopped

2 garlic cloves, peeled and crushed

4 thick slices veal, on the bone

all-purpose flour for coating

2 tbsp olive oil

8 tomatoes, skinned and chopped

½ cup dry white wine

1 cup beef broth (page 254)

3 bay leaves

sea salt and ground black pepper

1 tbsp butter, mixed with 2 tbsp
  all-purpose flour

gremolata

4 tbsp chopped flat-leaf parsley

1 tbsp finely grated lemon zest

1 garlic clove, peeled and crushed

1 oil-marinated anchovy, finely
  chopped

1 Preheat the oven to 350°F.

2 Melt the butter in a frying pan and cook the carrot, onions, celery and garlic gently for 5 minutes, or until they have softened. Remove from the pan and place in an ovenproof dish.

3 Coat the veal in flour. Heat the olive oil in the frying pan and cook the veal pieces until golden on each side. Remove from the pan and arrange over the vegetables in the casserole dish.

4 Add the tomatoes to the frying pan and cook, stirring constantly, for 5 minutes. Blend in the wine, broth, bay leaves and season to taste. Bring to a boil and simmer for 5 minutes. Whisk in the butter mixture and pour over the meat and vegetables.

5 Cover the casserole dish, and braise in the oven for 1½ hours, or until the meat is cooked through and tender.

6 For the *gremolata*, combine the parsley, lemon zest, garlic and anchovy. Sprinkle over the meat just before serving.

braised turkey with vegetables

tacchino alla cacciatora

This hunter-style stew – substantial and delicious – is based on a speciality of Mario at the *Montagliari trattoria* in Chianti. He serves it with roast potatoes with rosemary.

serves 6-8

1 oz dried *porcini*

2¾lb skinless, boneless turkey breast and thighs

2¾ tbsp unsalted butter

2 tbsp extra virgin olive oil

1 small sprig fresh rosemary

1 garlic clove, peeled and thinly sliced

3 bay leaves

2 medium onions, peeled and cut into 1-inch chunks

4 medium carrots, peeled and cut into 1-inch chunks

2 celery stalks, cut into 1-inch chunks

½ tsp each of chopped fresh marjoram, sage and thyme

sea salt and freshly ground black pepper

2 tbsp all-purpose flour

1 cup dry white wine

1 x 14.50-oz can diced tomatoes

1 cup chicken broth (see page 253)

1 Preheat the oven to 400°F.

2 Soak the *porcini* in water for 15 minutes. Lift them out of the soaking liquid, strain (keeping the liquid) and coarsely chop. Cut the turkey into pieces roughly 2 x 3 inches.

3 Melt the butter and oil together in a large, heavy-based ovenproof sauté pan over medium-to-high heat. Add the turkey and the sprig of rosemary, and brown the turkey on all sides. Add the garlic and bay leaves and cook until the garlic is golden. Stir in the onions, carrots and celery, sprinkle with the herbs, and season with salt and pepper to taste. Sprinkle in the flour and stir until dissolved. Stir in the wine, tomatoes, chopped *porcini* and their liquid, and half of the broth.

4 Bring to a boil and transfer the pan to the oven. Bake uncovered for 35-40 minutes, or until the turkey is cooked through. If the sauce becomes too thick, stir in some of the remaining broth. Remove the bay leaves and the rosemary sprig before serving.

Muscat grapes are my favorite if you can find them for this dish. This is based on a recipe from the *Agriturismo La Luna e il Falò* in Piedmont, in a village called Canelli. The Italian name of the *trattoria* is taken from the title of a novel by Cesare Pavese, meaning "the moon and the bonfires."

braised duck with grapes
anitra all'uva

serves 4

1 whole duck, about 4lb

4 tbsp olive oil

sea salt and freshly ground black
  pepper

1 medium onion, peeled and cut
  into small chunks

1 celery stalk, cut into small chunks

3 tbsp chopped mixed fresh herb
  leaves, such as oregano,
  rosemary, sage and thyme

3 small fresh bay leaves

⅔ cup dry white wine

10½ oz mixed seedless green
  and red grapes

1 Remove the liver and gizzards from the cavity of the duck and reserve them for another use. Rinse the duck inside and out and dry it well. Heat half the olive oil in a large casserole dish over medium-to-high heat. Add the duck and brown evenly on all sides. Transfer the duck to a platter and drain off the fat in the casserole dish.

2 When the duck has cooled, season the cavity with salt and pepper and fill it with half of the onion and celery and 2 tsp of the chopped herbs. Rub the surface of the duck with an additional 2 tsp of the herbs and season.

3 Heat the remaining olive oil in the casserole dish over medium heat. Add the duck and scatter all around it the remaining onion and celery and the bay leaves. Cook,

stirring the vegetables often, until they are lightly golden – about 10 minutes. Pour over the wine and bring it to a boil. Partially cover the pan and simmer for 1 hour, turning the duck every 20 minutes. Stir 10 green and 10 red grapes into the casserole dish and simmer, covered, for another 30 minutes, or until the duck is fully cooked.

4 Transfer the duck from the casserole dish to a shallow platter and cover it with foil. Discard the bay leaves and purée the contents of the casserole dish in a food mill or in a food processor. Pour the sauce back into the casserole dish. Simmer the sauce briskly until it has thickened. Stir in the remaining grapes and herbs. Simmer for 2-3 minutes and season with salt and pepper.

5 Cut the duck into small serving pieces, removing the skin if desired. Arrange the duck on a shallow serving plate, spoon the sauce and the grapes over it, and serve immediately.

| meat & poultry

savoy chicken stew with umbrian flatbread
spezzatino di pollo con torta al testo

This dish is a classic speciality of the *trattorias* that surround Trasimeno, the principal lake in land-locked Umbria, but this recipe actually came to me from Ezio and Maria Anghinetti, who ran the *Trattoria La Maesta* near Parma. Ezio originally hails from Umbria, though, thus the local *torta al testo* – crisp flatbread baked on the floor of the hearth (the bread can also be baked on terracotta tiles in a conventional oven). Select a free-range chicken that is meaty and then ask the butcher to cut the chicken into small pieces using a meat saw, to avoid splintered bones.

serves 4
flatbread
1¼ cups warm water
1¼ tbsp fresh yeast
3 tsp sea salt
3¼ cups white bread flour
olive oil

1 To make the flatbread, mix 1 tbsp of the warm water with the fresh yeast to dissolve. Mix the salt and flour together in a large bowl. Make a well in the middle, and add the dissolved yeast, 1 tbsp oil and the remaining water to form a damp ball.

2 Turn out on to a board and knead for about 7 minutes to make a soft ball of dough, adding more flour if necessary. Transfer the dough to a large, well-oiled bowl. Rub the dough against the bowl to coat it with oil. Cover the bowl with a damp dish-towel and let it rise until double its size, about 1 hour.

3 While the dough is rising, arrange terracotta tiles or a pizza stone on the center shelf of the oven. Preheat the oven to 400°F. Allow 30 minutes for the oven and the tiles to preheat.

4 When the dough is ready, turn it out on to the lightly floured board and knead for 2 minutes to force out any

stew

1 free-range chicken,
   3lb 10 oz, cut into 18 pieces

1 small garlic clove, peeled and
   finely chopped

½ medium onion, peeled and
   coarsely chopped

1 small carrot, peeled and
   coarsely chopped

½ celery stalk, coarsely chopped

½ tsp coarsely chopped fresh
   rosemary leaves

⅓ cup extra virgin olive oil

2 small fresh hot red chilies,
   seeded and chopped

sea salt and freshly ground black
   pepper

¾ cup dry white wine

9fl oz canned tomatoes,
   diced

air bubbles. Cover the dough and let it rest for 5 minutes. Divide the dough into four equal pieces. Work with one piece of dough at a time, flouring the remaining pieces and covering them with the damp dish-towel. Flatten the dough slightly. Lightly flour a ridged wooden rolling pin and roll out the dough to ¼ inch thick. Prick with a fork and transfer the dough to a floured pizza peel (the piece of wood that you put the pizza into the oven with) or a rimless baking sheet.

5 Slide the dough directly on to the hot tile. Bake for 7–9 minutes, or until golden around the edge and puffy. Cool on a cooling rack. Roll out and bake the remaining pieces of dough in the same way.

6 To make the chicken stew, heat a large, heavy-based sauté pan over medium-to-high heat and add the chicken pieces. Cover the pan and cook, turning the pieces from time to time, until the chicken has rendered all of its fat and water and has become golden in colour – about 15 minutes. Remove the chicken and drain off both the fat and liquid.

7 Meanwhile, combine the garlic, onion, carrot, celery and rosemary and food process to make a coarse purée.

8 Return the chicken to the pan and pour the olive oil over it. Add the chilies, season with salt to taste, and spoon the puréed vegetables over the chicken. Simmer, covered, for 20 minutes. Pour in the wine and simmer for 15 minutes more. Stir in the tomatoes and simmer, covered, for 15 minutes more. If the mixture appears dry at any time, reduce the heat and add extra water. Taste and season if necessary. Serve the stew with the flatbread.

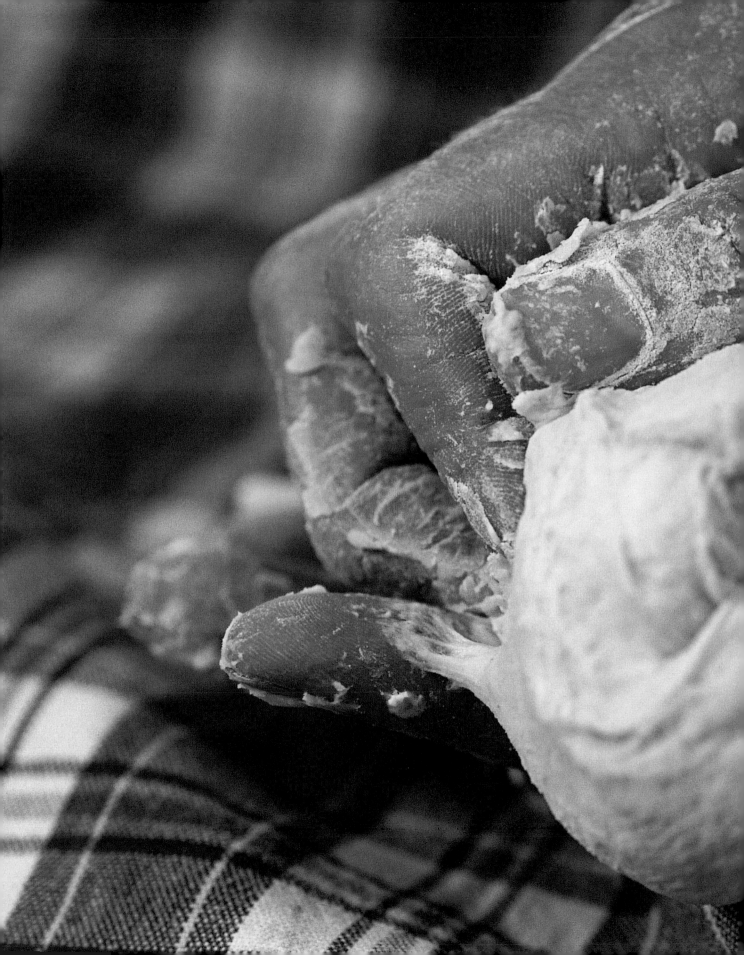

breads & pizzas

basic pizza dough
impasto per pizza

Pizzas are quintessential *trattoria* fare. This recipe will yield two
individual-sized pizzas, approximately 10 inches in diameter. Extra
dough balls can be frozen for up to two months.

makes 2 x 10-inch pizza bases

1¼ tbsp fresh yeast or 1½ tsp
   fast-action dried yeast

3⅓ tbsp room temperature
   water

1¾ cups white unbleached bread
flour

½ tsp sea salt

3⅓ tbsp olive oil, plus extra
   for greasing

semolina for sprinkling

1 Blend the fresh yeast with a little of the water. Sift the flour and
salt together into a large bowl. Make a well in the center and
add the oil, yeast liquid and some of the water. Mix with a
wooden spoon, gradually adding the remaining water to form a
soft dough. If using fast-action dried yeast, mix in with the
flour, then add the water as above.

2 Turn the dough out on to a lightly floured surface and knead
vigorously for 10 minutes, until it is soft and satiny. Don't be
afraid of adding more flour. Place in a lightly oiled large bowl,
then turn the dough around to coat with the oil. Cover the
bowl with a clean dish-towel and leave in a warm place for
1½ hours, or until the dough has doubled in size.

3 Preheat the oven to 400°F. In the bottom of the oven,
preheat two oiled baking sheets or a terracotta pizza stone.
Knock down the dough with your knuckles, then turn on to a
lightly floured surface and knead for 2-3 minutes to knock out
the air bubbles. Divide the dough in half.

4 On a lightly floured surface, preferably marble, roll out the
pieces of dough very, very thinly until 10-12 inches in diameter
(they should be as thin as a paper napkin folded in four). Lift
each pizza on to a cold baking sheet sprinkled generously with
semolina. Add your chosen topping. Bake for 20-25 minutes,
until the crusts are golden.

uncooked tomato sauce for pizza
salsa di pomodoro crudo

This is one of the most basic sauces in the Italian culinary vocabulary. It is very simple to make, and tastes wonderful with pasta as well as on pizza – but the hour's marination is crucial for the development of a full flavor.

enough for 2 pizzas
1lb 10 oz fresh plum tomatoes
6 fresh basil leaves, torn
sea salt and freshly ground black
  pepper

1 Skin the tomatoes by first cutting a little nick through the skin, then plunging them into boiling water for a few seconds. Remove with a slotted spoon and plunge into cold water.

2 Slip the tomato skins off, then seed and chop the tomato flesh finely.

3 Simply mix the tomato with the basil and some salt and pepper to taste. Set aside for 1 hour before using.

pizza with spicy tomato, olives and capers
pizza puttanesca

This is my spicy pizza. It gets its zest from the famous southern Italian *puttanesca* sauce, to which hot red pepper has been added.

serves 2

2 pizza dough bases (see page 182)

6 tbsp uncooked tomato sauce (see page 183)

1 garlic clove, peeled and chopped

4 oil-marinated anchovies

15 Ligurian black olives, pitted

1 tsp salted capers, soaked and dried

1-2 tsp dried chili (*peperoncino*)

freshly ground black pepper (optional)

1 Preheat the oven to 400°F and oil and preheat large baking sheets or preheat a baking stone.

2 Spread the tomato sauce over the pizza dough. Arrange the garlic, anchovies, olives, capers and chili on top.

3 Slide on to the hot baking sheets or a baking stone and then into the oven. Bake until the crust is crisp and golden – about 20-25 minutes. Serve with freshly ground black pepper if desired.

white pizza with ham and cheese
pizza bianca con prosciutto e fontina

This is in the spirit of a focaccia, a sort of glorified sandwich. If you can't get fontina, try Swiss cheese or Gruyère. They're not Italian, obviously, but give the same texture and nutty flavor as fontina.

serves 2

2 pizza dough bases (see page 182)

3½ oz fontina cheese, cubed

3½ oz mozzarella, cubed

a handful of arugula leaves, stems trimmed, coarsely chopped

1 plum tomato, diced

2 tbsp extra virgin olive oil

5 paper-thin slices Parma ham (*prosciutto di Parma*)

sea salt and freshly ground black pepper

1 Preheat the oven to 400°F and oil and preheat baking sheets or preheat a baking stone.

2 Mix the fontina and mozzarella cheeses together, then spread on the pizza dough. Slide on to the hot baking sheets or baking stone and then into the preheated oven. Bake until the cheese is bubbly – about 20-25 minutes.

3 Remove from the oven, then cover the pizza with the arugula and tomato and drizzle with olive oil. Top with the *prosciutto* and season with salt and pepper.

trattoria dell'orso

Umbria is the green heart of Italy, one of the few regions in the country that does not have a coastline. It's dominated by lakes, however, of which the largest is Trasimeno, and a prime ingredient of the many *trattorias* in the region is freshwater fish, for instance pike.

The food is hearty and rich, with a lot of meat: the city of Norcia is famous for its pork and pork products, in particular the local *porchetta*, a whole roast pig. Black truffles feature in the cooking in season, and Umbrian olive oil is delicious.

Umbria is beautiful, with its myriad hill towns, among them the capital Perugia, and exploring the local food through the many local *trattorias* is a wonderful way of getting to know the region. One of the best is in Orvieto, the *Trattoria dell' Orso*, which is next door to the Cathedral and many other architectural delights.

The food is classically and carefully prepared, and the atmosphere is relaxed – with the occasional touch of flamboyance. It is popular locally, but also with visitors from further afield.

This is a very aromatic and flavorful pizza, particularly suited to the cold months of the year, when wild mushrooms are in season. I worked once in a *trattoria* in Umbria for a while, and noticed that this one, or one very similar, was by far the most popular. The dried porcini mushrooms enrich the texture and flavor.

pizza with wild mushrooms
pizza con funghi selvatici

serves 2

2 pizza dough bases
(see page 182)

1 tbsp olive oil

½ garlic clove, peeled and
chopped

6 oz fresh wild mushrooms,
cleaned and coarsely chopped

½ oz dried *porcini*, soaked in
water for 30 minutes

a handful of fresh flat-leaf parsley,
roughly chopped

4 tbsp uncooked tomato sauce (see
page 183)

5½ oz mozzarella, cubed

freshly ground black pepper

1 Preheat the oven to 400°F and oil and preheat two baking sheets or preheat a stone.

2 In a frying pan, heat the olive oil, then add the garlic and sauté over medium heat until lightly golden. Add the mushrooms and drained *porcini* and sauté for 5-7 minutes over medium heat. Sprinkle with parsley.

3 Spread the tomato sauce over the pizza dough bases. Top with the mozzarella and a layer of sautéed mushrooms.

4 Slide on to the hot baking sheets or baking stone and bake until bubbly – about 20-25 minutes. Serve with a twist of black pepper.

pizza with four cheeses

pizza ai quattro formaggi

This is a classic pizza. It does not call for tomato sauce. I like this combination of cheeses because the spicy and sweet flavors are well balanced, but you can substitute any Italian cheeses you like.

serves 2

2 pizza dough bases (see page 183)

2 oz fontina cheese, cubed

3 oz mozzarella, cubed

2 oz Gorgonzola, cubed

2 oz *provolone*, shredded

freshly ground black pepper

1 Preheat the oven to 400°F and oil and preheat large baking sheets or preheat a baking stone.

2 Cover each quarter of each dough with a different variety of cheese.

3 Slide on to a heated pizza stone or baking sheets and bake until the crust is golden and the cheeses are bubbly – about 20-25 minutes. Serve with pepper if desired.

basic focaccine

impasto per focaccine

This rich, yeasty bread is a relation of focaccia, but is much thinner, lighter and crunchier. It can be baked and eaten by itself with soups and is wonderful with a final sprinkling of olive oil and herbs. It is also delicious when stuffed and baked as a sandwich and is eaten like this extensively in *trattorias* in Rome and Naples. See the following pages for a few filling suggestions. If you ever have any dough left over, wrap it in plastic wrap and store in the fridge, it will keep for a couple of days.

makes 4

1¼ tbsp fresh yeast (fresh is best
 – easier on the digestive tract)

1 cup room temperature
 water

3 cups bread flour

2 tsp fine salt

1 tbsp olive oil, plus extra for
 brushing

sea salt and freshly ground black
 pepper

1 tbsp extra virgin olive oil

1 Combine the yeast with a little of the warm water, and stir until dissolved. In a bowl, combine the flour, remaining water, fine salt, yeast and oil. Turn out on to a floured board and knead for 12 minutes, until smooth and elastic. Cover with a damp dish-towel and allow to rest for 12 minutes.

2 Divide the dough into four equal portions and shape each into a ball. Stretch each ball into a ½-inch thick x 9-inch diameter circle and place on a baking tray. Cover with a damp dish-towel and allow to rest for 1½ hours at room temperature, or until doubled in size.

3 Flatten the dough with your hands and use your thumb to form little pockets. Brush the *focaccine* with a little olive oil and sprinkle with sea salt and black pepper. Cover and allow to rise for another hour. Preheat the oven to 400ºF. Bake for 10-12 minutes, until golden. Sprinkle with the extra virgin olive oil as it comes out of the oven. Cool.

breacs & pizzas

goat's cheese and grilled vegetable focaccina
focaccina di caprino e verdure grigliate

This delicious *focaccine* sandwich is a typical lunchtime dish
in many *trattorias*. Try to find really good extra virgin olive oil
for this dish.

fills a 9-inch *focaccine* and serves 2

1 cooked *focaccine* (see page 193)

2 fine zucchini slices, cut lengthwise

2 fine eggplant slices

1 slice red pepper

1 slice yellow pepper

a handful of fresh flat-leaf parsley, finely chopped

4 tbsp fine extra virgin olive oil, plus extra for sprinkling

4½ oz fresh tasty goat's cheese

3-4 sun-dried tomatoes, drained and cut into strips

sea salt and freshly ground black pepper

1 Marinate the vegetables and parsley in the olive oil for 1 hour.

2 Preheat the oven to 300°F.

3 Grill the vegetables at medium to high heat until lightly browned, either under the broiler or on a ridged cast-iron grill pan. Turn after 2-3 minutes.

4 Cut the *focaccine* in half horizontally. Spread one side with goat's cheese, top with grilled vegetables and sun-dried tomatoes, and season. Place on a baking sheet, put the top on and bake for 3-4 minutes only.

5 Sprinkle with extra virgin olive oil and halve or cut into wedges.

soppressata, zucchini, sun-dried tomato and provolone focaccina

focaccina di soppressata, zucchini, pomodori secchi e provolone

A filling *focaccina* with wonderfully strong flavors.

fills a 9-inch *focaccine* and serves 2

1 cooked *focaccina* (see page 193)

3½ oz *soppressata* or salami

2 oz zucchini, finely sliced
  and grilled

4 sun-dried tomatoes, finely cut

3½ oz provolone, finely
  sliced

1 Preheat the oven to 300°F.

2 Cut the *focaccina* in half horizontally. Cover one half with the *soppressata*, the grilled zucchini, sun-dried tomatoes and provolone. Place on a baking sheet.

3 Put the top on and bake for 3-4 minutes only. Halve or cut into wedges and serve immediately.

stracchino cheese and truffle oil focaccine
focaccina di stracchino e olio tartufato

The addition of truffle oil makes this *focaccine* sandwich a real treat. Serve it cut up into wedges.

fills a 9-inch *focaccine* and serves 2

1 cooked *focaccine* (see page 193)

7 oz fresh, soft *stracchino* cheese

sea salt and freshly ground black pepper

2 tbsp truffle oil

1 Preheat the oven to 300°F.

2 Cut the *focaccine* in half horizontally. Spread one half with cheese, season with salt and pepper and place on a baking sheet.

3 Put the top on and bake for 3-4 minutes only, or until the cheese has melted.

4 Sprinkle the inside with the truffle oil, halve or cut into wedges and serve immediately.

breads & pizzas

bresaola, mascarpone and arugula focaccine

focaccina di bresaola, mascarpone e rucola

fills a 9-inch *focaccine* and serves 2

1 cooked *focaccine* (see page 193)

3 oz Mascarpone cheese

1 celery stalk, chopped

1 tbsp chopped fresh chives

sea salt and freshly ground black pepper

4 thin slices bresaola

a handful of arugula leaves

1 Preheat the oven to 300°F.

2 Combine the mascarpone, celery, chives and seasoning and mix well.

3 Cut the *focaccine* in half horizontally. Spread the mixture on one half of the *focaccine*, add the bresaola and the top half of the *focaccine*, and bake for 3-4 minutes only.

4 Stuff the *focaccine* with arugula, halve or cut into wedges, and serve.

ricotta flatbread
schiacciata con ricotta

This is a Tuscan recipe, from a charming *trattoria* owned by *Gianfranco Vissani*, after its owner. His bread is memorable, and the *trattoria* is well worth a visit. Any good *trattoria* will make its own bread, of course, and this would be a morning ritual. You could add anything to this bread – crispy bits of pancetta, walnuts, raisins and figs, for instance – but the ricotta is a basic, giving the bread a wonderful texture. In fact this bread can be as interesting as you are!

makes 2 loaves, serves 8
1¼ tbsp fresh yeast
1 cup warm water
8½ oz fresh ricotta cheese,
   allowed to sit at room
   temperature for 15 minutes
3 tsp sea salt
a pinch of fennel seeds
3-3¼ cups bread flour
olive oil

egg wash
1 large egg yolk
1 tsp water

1 To make the bread dough, dissolve the yeast in some of the water in a large bowl. Stir in the ricotta, salt and fennel seeds. Add the flour little by little, using only enough flour to make a soft dough.

2 Turn the dough out on to a lightly floured work surface, and knead for 10 minutes, incorporating more flour if necessary to keep it from sticking. The dough should be smooth and tender. Transfer to a large bowl and drizzle about 2 tbsp olive oil over it. Rub the oil over the dough's surface, cover the bowl with a damp cloth, and leave for 1 hour, until the dough has doubled in size.

3   Preheat the oven to 400°F, and oil a large baking sheet. When the dough is ready, turn it out on to the work surface and knead for 2 minutes. Flour the dough lightly, wrap in plastic wrap, and let rest for 5 minutes.

5   Flatten the dough with a rolling pin and shape it into a 13 x 8-inch oval. Transfer to the greased baking sheet. Cut a 7-inch long slit lengthwise through the center of the dough to the baking sheet, but do not cut the ends. Spread the split open slightly. Cover the dough with a dish-towel and let it rest for 15 minutes more.

6   Make the egg wash by beating the egg yolk and water in a small bowl. Brush the egg wash over the surface of the dough. Bake the bread on the center shelf of the oven for 25-30 minutes or until rich brown and cooked through. Turn the bread on its side and knock on the bottom. If done, the bread will make a hollow sound. Cool the bread on a cooling rack. I break it in half before serving.

breads & pizzas

desserts & cakes

baked figs with hazelnuts and fromage frais
fichi al forno con noccioline e fromage frais

This is the sort of dessert a *trattoria* in the south serves in late summer.
Italy's best figs come from the south, around the Naples area, having had
all summer to ripen in the hot sun. I use fromage frais, as it is lighter
than mascarpone, so that you can appreciate the fragrance of the figs.
Frangelico goes beautifully with figs, but you could use vermouth instead.

serves 4

12 ripe fresh figs

**1 cup shelled hazelnuts,
toasted and halved**

3 tbsp mild runny honey

**3 tbsp Frangelico (hazelnut
liqueur)**

4 oz fromage frais

1 Preheat the oven to 400°F. Cut a tiny slice off the bottom
of each fig so that it will sit stably. Make two cuts down
through their tops, about 1 inch deep, at right angles to
one another. Ease each fig open, squeezing their middles
to make the "petals" open out a bit.

2 Mix most of the nuts with the honey, Frangelico and
fromage frais. Spoon this into the opened-out figs and
arrange them in a baking dish.

3 Bake for 15 minutes, until the cheese is bubbling. Sprinkle
over the remaining toasted hazelnuts and serve.

fresh fruit tarts

tortino di frutta fresca

Tarts such as this would be made daily in most *trattorias*, using seasonal fruit, often picked from their own *orto* or kitchen garden. The combination of fruit here is not classically Italian, perhaps, but it works very well. You could also try raspberries, strawberries and blueberries, for instance. The *crème pâtissière* is very Italian (despite its French name): it is used in celebration cakes and tarts, and in pastries for breakfast. And the almond pastry here is a classic.

serves 4

Italian almond pastry (makes about 14 oz)

1⅛ cups all-purpose flour

a pinch of salt

⅓ cup superfine granulated sugar

½ cup ground almonds

⅓ cup unsalted butter, cubed

a few drops of vanilla extract

1 medium egg, beaten

crème pâtissière

3 medium egg yolks

½ cup superfine granulated sugar

¼ cup all-purpose flour

1¼ cups milk

1 tsp vanilla extract

1 medium egg white

⅔ cup whipping cream

topping

4 oz cherries, halved and pitted

4 oz green and/or red grapes, halved and seeded

2 kiwi fruit, peeled and sliced

apricot glaze

8 oz apricot conserve

1 tbsp Kirsch

1   For the pastry, sift flour, salt and sugar into a bowl, then mix in the almonds. Rub in the butter until the mixture resembles fine breadcrumbs. Make a well in the center, add vanilla and egg, mix with a round-bladed knife to form a dough. Knead on lightly floured surface for a few seconds until smooth. Wrap in plastic wrap. Chill for 30 minutes.

2   For the *crème pâtissière*, whisk the egg yolks and 1¾ tbsp of the sugar in a bowl until pale and thick. Fold in the flour. Put the milk and vanilla in a pan and bring almost to a boil. Gently whisk the hot milk into the egg and flour, then strain through a sieve back into the pan. Cook the custard over a gentle heat, stirring, until it thickens. Pour the hot custard into a clean bowl, then cover closely with plastic wrap. Allow to cool completely but not to set too firmly. Whisk the egg white until stiff, then gradually whisk in the remaining sugar. Whip the cream until thick. Whisk the cooled custard until smooth, then gradually fold in the egg white followed by the cream. Cover and chill.

3   Roll out the pastry on a lightly floured surface and cut out 5-inch circles with a round cutter and use to line 4-inch greased individual tart pans. Trim the edges and prick the base of each tartlet, then place the lined tart pans on a baking sheet and freeze for at least 15 minutes.

4   Preheat the oven to 400°F. Move the pastry cases straight from the freezer into the oven and bake for 15 minutes. Allow to cool a little in their pans, then transfer to a wire rack to cool. Mix the conserve and Kirsch in a small pan and heat to melt. Brush over the inside of each pastry case, reserving left-over glaze. Divide the custard equally between the pastry cases and spread it evenly. Arrange the cherries, grapes and kiwi fruit on top. Reheat the remaining glaze and brush it over. Serve soon after.

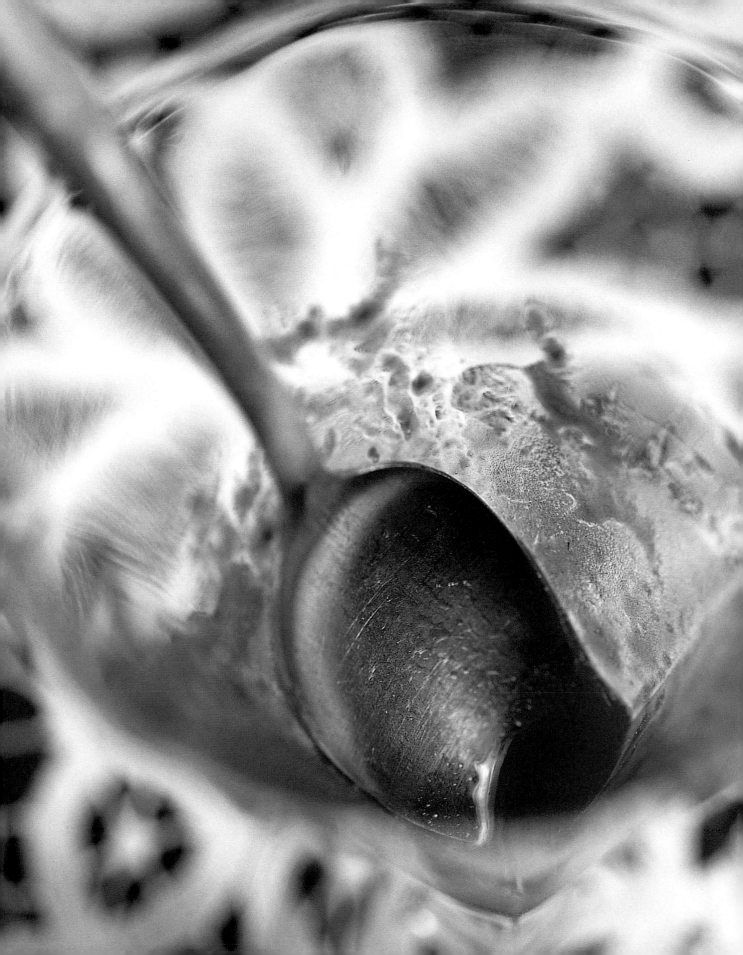

raspberry sorbet

sorbetto di lamponi

Italians love iced food, particularly in the south, where sorbets or ice-cream are wonderfully refreshing in the exhausting heat of the day. *Trattorias* would make *sorbetti* like this, using fruit from the kitchen garden or *orto*, probably grown, tended and made by the *mama della casa* (the house). Loganberries or blackberries may be used instead, in season, for a richer color and sharper flavor.

serves 6-8
1⅛ **cups granulated sugar**
⅔ **cup water**
1lb **fresh raspberries**
juice of 1 large lemon

1 Put the sugar in a saucepan with the water and heat gently until the sugar has dissolved. Bring to a boil and boil for 1 minute. Remove from the heat and allow to cool.

2 Press the raspberries through a coarse sieve, or purée in a blender or food processor, then sieve to remove the seeds.

3 Blend the raspberry purée, lemon juice and sugar syrup together. Make in an ice-cream maker if you have one, or pour into a shallow container and freeze for about 3½ hours, until softly frozen, removing from the freezer every hour and whisking well.

4 Spoon into chilled glasses and serve.

vanilla ice-cream with hot espresso
affogato al caffè

As a substitute for plain coffee or espresso at the end of a *trattoria* or family meal, this dessert is always well received and takes next to no time to prepare. "*Affogato*" means "drowned," and many people believe that adding a "drowning" scoop of ice-cream to strong coffee tames the effect of the caffeine. I recommend this on a hot day when you need a kick-start and don't feel much like eating.

serves 1

2 oz bittersweet chocolate,
  broken into pieces

3 scoops vanilla ice-cream

1 little cup hot espresso coffee,
  about 3⅓ tbsp, as strong as
  you like it

1 Put the chocolate in a bowl over a pan of simmering water (which mustn't touch the chocolate), and melt, stirring occasionally.

2 Put the ice-cream in a serving bowl. Pour the hot espresso over the ice-cream, followed by the hot melted chocolate. Eat immediately.

Emilia-Romagna is the prime gastronomic region of Italy, as it produces so many famous and flavorful foods – among them Parma ham, Parmesan cheese and the wonderful balsamic vinegars of Modena. In this region, people think, talk and fantasize about food more than anywhere else in Italy, from morning to night asking each other what they are going to eat, how they will prepare it and what they will serve it with.

The food is rich because the land is so fertile, and in and around Bologna, the capital, there are many *trattorias* that specialize in regional cooking. Prime among these must be the *Osteria di Rubbiara*, where the food is simple, delicious, traditional, rustic and very puristic.

Out in the countryside, and quite difficult to locate, *Osteria di Rubbiara* is well worth making the effort to find, not least because of its wines (on which an *osteria*, rather than a *trattoria*, will concentrate) and its superb home-made balsamic vinegar.

osteria di rubbiara

coffee pudding

budino al caffè

This is a simple and refreshing dessert that has been served by my family for generations. You'd probably find something similar in a *trattoria*.

serves 6

7 tbsp superfine granulated sugar

1 tsp fresh lemon juice

1 tbsp water

¾ cup brewed strong espresso coffee, cooled

5 large eggs

2½ cups whipping cream

1 Place 2 tbsp of the sugar, the lemon juice and water in a small heavy-based saucepan. Cook over medium heat until the mixture turns a pale caramel color. Immediately pour the caramel into a shallow 10-inch ring mould, tilting it in all directions to distribute the caramel over the bottom and sides. Continue to tilt until the caramel has hardened. Let the mould cool for 30 minutes.

2 Meanwhile, combine the cooled espresso and the remaining sugar in a bowl and mix well. Beat the eggs one at a time and add them to the espresso, mixing well.

3 Preheat the oven to 350°F.

4 Pour the coffee and egg mixture into the mould and place the mould in a large pan filled with enough hot water to come halfway up the sides of the mould. Bake for 1 hour.

5 Allow the pudding to cool for 1 hour, then unmould on to a serving plate. Whip the cream and use to fill the center of the ring, then serve. I sometimes serve this with melted chocolate sauce and strawberries.

frangelico chocolate pudding with white chocolate sauce

budino di cioccolato frangelico con salsa di cioccolato bianco

The fragrant Frangelico liqueur goes well with many fruits, and it is wonderful with chocolate. Baked puddings such as this would be part of the repertoire of many a *trattoria*, and at home a dish such as this could quickly become a regular dinner-party or family-lunch dessert. For a start, it's so blissfully straightforward to cook!

serves 10

13 oz bitter chocolate, broken into pieces

1½ cups unsalted butter, plus extra for greasing

8 large eggs, separated

3¾ cups shelled hazelnuts, toasted and finely ground

1½ cups confectioner's sugar

2 tbsp Frangelico (a hazelnut liqueur)

sauce

6 oz white chocolate, broken into pieces

2 tbsp Frangelico

1 Preheat the oven to 350°F, and grease 10 ramekins. Place on a baking tray.

2 Melt the butter and chocolate together in a bowl over a pan of hot water. Cool for 5 minutes. Beat the egg yolks and add them to the mixture, stirring on very low heat. Add the ground hazelnuts, confectioner's sugar and liqueur. Remove from the heat and cool.

3 Whip the egg whites until stiff, then gently fold into the mixture. Divide the mixture between the ramekins and bake for 25 minutes.

4 Shortly before the end of the cooking time, melt the white chocolate with the Frangelico in a bowl over a pan of simmering water. Unmould the puddings and serve on a pool of the warm white chocolate sauce.

chocolate cake santini

torta di cioccolata santini

This chocolate cake is dedicated to my friend Santini, who used to work on my father's farm. It was he who taught me to appreciate combining chocolate and prunes, and the cake is voluptuously rich and indulgent.

serves 20

unsalted butter for greasing

7 oz prunes

4 tbsp Grand Marnier

1 vanilla pod, split lengthways

28 oz good quality dark
  chocolate (80% cocoa solids)

3½ cups whipping cream

confectioner's sugar to sprinkle

1 Butter a 2½-inch deep x 9-inch diameter springform pan, and line with parchment paper, bottom and sides. Reserve 12 prunes to decorate the cake. Halve and pit the rest, roughly chop them and put them in a small bowl with the Grand Marnier and the split vanilla pod. Leave to macerate for 1 hour, stirring occasionally. Remove the pod.

2 Reserve 2 oz of the chocolate, and put the remainder, in small pieces, in a heatproof bowl over a pan of simmering water. Do not let the bottom of the bowl touch the water. Leave for 15-20 minutes, stirring occasionally, until melted.

3 Remove the chocolate from the heat, then gently stir in the cream, soaked prunes and any extra liquid. Pour the mixture into the prepared cake pan, smooth over the surface with a palette knife, cover with plastic wrap and refrigerate for at least 6 hours or overnight.

4 When the cake has set, remove it from its pan, discard the parchment paper, and slide onto serving plate. Melt the reserved chocolate over a pan of simmering water for 1 minute and spoon into small plastic bag. Twist neck of the bag to push the filling into one corner. Using scissors, snip off a small piece from one corner of the bag. In a zigzag motion, pipe the chocolate across the cake. Serve chilled, decorated with pitted prunes and confectioner's sugar.

hazelnut semifreddo with chocolate and frangelico sauce

semifreddo con nocciole e salsa frangelico

Every *trattoria* has a selection of ice-creams. A *semifreddo* is a more elegant version of a *gelato*.

serves 8

semifreddo

1 cup shelled hazelnuts, toasted

1½ cups superfine granulated sugar

2 tbsp water

1⅛ cup whipping cream

3 large egg whites

3 tbsp Frangelico (a hazelnut liqueur)

sauce

2 tbsp whipping cream

2 tbsp Frangelico (a hazelnut liqueur)

3½ oz bitter chocolate, coarsely chopped

½ tsp pure vanilla extract

a pinch of sea salt

1 Line eight ramekins with plastic wrap, leaving a 3-inch overhang. Finely chop the nuts. Put half the sugar into a small saucepan, stir in the water and bring to a boil over a moderate heat. Simmer, brushing down the sides of the saucepan with a wet pastry brush, until a deep caramel forms – about 5 minutes. Remove the pan from the heat and, using a wooden spoon, stir in the nuts. Immediately scrape the mixture on to an oiled baking sheet and let it cool until it is hard. Break the praline into small pieces and transfer to a food processor. Grind to a coarse powder.

2 In a stainless-steel bowl, whip the cream until it holds firm peaks, then refrigerate. In a large stainless-steel bowl, beat the egg whites until they hold firm, glossy peaks – towards the end of the whisking time, whisk in the rest of the sugar little by little. Using a spatula, fold in the praline powder, then the cream and 3 tbsp of Frangelico.

3 Spoon the *semifreddo* into the ramekins, pressing down to remove any air pockets. Cover with the overhanging plastic wrap and freeze until firm – about 2 hours. In a small saucepan, bring the 2 tbsp cream to a boil over moderate heat. Remove the pan from the heat and stir in the chopped chocolate, vanilla, salt and Frangelico and let cool. Chill the sauce for 1 hour, then serve over the semifreddo.

pistachio and hazelnut torte
torta di pistacchio e nocciole

This is a cake for celebrations – for a christening, Holy Communion festivities or birthdays. You won't often find *trattorias* offering such big fancy cakes on their menus, but they can often be pre-ordered.

serves 12

pastry

1½ cups all-purpose flour

a pinch of salt

½ cup confectioner's sugar

½ cup shelled pistachio nuts, skinned and fairly finely ground

⅓ cup shelled hazelnuts, skinned and fairly finely ground

1 cup unsalted butter, cut into pieces

filling

2½ cups whipping cream

finely grated zest of 1 unwaxed orange

2 tbsp Grand Marnier

1 tbsp confectioner's sugar

4 oranges, peeled and segmented

to decorate

confectioner's sugar for sifting

chopped pistachio nuts

1 Preheat the oven to 350°F. For the pastry, sift the flour, salt and confectioner's sugar into a bowl, add the nuts and mix well. Rub in the butter, working the ingredients together gently until they form a ball. Cut the pastry into two equal pieces. Roll out each piece on a lightly floured surface into a circle a little smaller than 10 inches.

2 Place each pastry circle in a 10-inch fluted quiche pan, then press the pastry gently over the base of the pan until it fits. Smooth the pastry with the back of a spoon, but do not stretch it. Prick with a fork and freeze for 15 minutes. Remove straight from the freezer to the oven and bake for 30-35 minutes, until the pastry is lightly brown. Instantly cut one of the circles into 12 triangular-shaped pieces. Allow to cool slightly, then move to wire racks to cool completely.

3 Whip the cream with the orange zest, Grand Marnier and confectioner's sugar until it holds soft peaks. Place the pastry circle on a plate, spread ¾ of the cream over it. Arrange the orange segments over the cream. Whip the remaining cream again until it is thick enough to pipe. Pipe 12 large rosettes on top of the fruit about 1 inch from the edge. Arrange the triangular-shaped pieces of pastry on top of the *torte*, placing them at an angle, each one supported by a rosette of cream. Sift confectioner's sugar lightly over the top and decorate with the nuts.

hazelnut meringue cake
torta di nocciole e meringa

This is another classic example of Italian home cooking. It is a delicious combination of nuts and fruit, with a base of crisp and light meringue. It's not complicated to make, and looks incredibly impressive.

serves 6-8

3 large egg whites

1½ cups superfine granulated sugar

½ cup shelled hazelnuts, skinned, toasted and finely chopped

1¼ cups whipping cream

12 oz fresh raspberries, hulled

to decorate

confectioner's sugar for sifting

finely chopped pistachio nuts for sprinkling

1 Preheat the oven to 275°F. Line two baking sheets with parchment paper, then draw an 8-inch circle on each one.

2 Whisk the egg whites until they are very stiff but not dry. Towards the end of the whisking time, add the sugar gradually, whisking well between each addition, until the meringue is stiff and very shiny. Carefully fold in the chopped hazelnuts.

3 Divide the meringue equally between the baking sheets, then spread neatly into the marked circles. With a palette knife, shape the top of one of the circles into swirls – this will be the top meringue. Bake for about 1½ hours, until dry. Turn the oven off and allow the meringue to cool in the oven.

4 Whip the cream until it holds soft peaks. Carefully remove the meringue from the parchment paper. Place the smooth meringue round on a large flat serving plate, then spread with the cream. Arrange the raspberries on top of the cream, then place the second meringue on top. Sift confectioner's sugar over the top of the cake and sprinkle with finely chopped pistachio nuts. Serve as soon as possible.

confetteria
cioccolateria

italian rice pudding
budino di riso italiano

The Veneto and Venice are particularly associated with rice, as the crop is grown extensively in the valley of the Po not far to the north. There are famous risottos and other savory rice dishes, as well as a few sweet dishes, which you would probably find in a local *trattoria*. You can serve this pudding on its own, or with poached peaches, plums, blackberries or indeed any fruit.

serves 4

$1\frac{1}{8}$ **cup arborio rice**

$1\frac{1}{4}$ **cups whole milk**

$1\frac{1}{4}$ **cups whipping cream**

1 vanilla pod, split in half
  lengthways

1 tsp vanilla extract

$\frac{1}{2}$ **tsp sea salt**

6 tbsp water

$1\frac{3}{4}$ **tbsp unsalted butter**

1 cup superfine granulated sugar

1 Put the rice in a medium-sized, heavy-based pan. Pour in the milk, cream, vanilla pod and extract, salt and water. Bring to a boil over medium heat, then turn down the flame until the milk is bubbling gently, just as you would for a risotto. Let it cook for 15-20 minutes. The rice will be soft when ready.

2 Add the butter, remove the vanilla pod, then stir in the sugar. When the sugar has dissolved the pudding is ready.

heart-shaped cookies
biscotti a forma di cuore

The Italians are famously passionate and romantic, and making cookies or other foods in heart shapes is very popular. I think these would be perfect for St Valentine's Day, for someone's birthday, or for part of a special occasion in the *trattoria* or at home. You can of course make the cookies any shape. Eat them with ice-cream, dip them into Vin Santo, or even eat them with a coffee in the afternoon as a *merenda*, or snack.

makes 20-24

⅔ cup unsalted butter,
  plus extra for greasing
1¼ cups superfine granulated
sugar, plus extra for sprinkling
1 large egg yolk, beaten
1⅔ cups all-purpose flour
finely grated zest of 1 unwaxed
  lemon
1 large egg white, lightly beaten
  with 1 tbsp water

1 Preheat the oven to 350°F. Grease two large baking sheets.

2 Cream together the butter and sugar until light and fluffy. Add the egg yolk and beat well, then stir in the flour and lemon zest.

3 Knead lightly and shape into a ball. Wrap in plastic wrap and chill slightly to make it firm and easier to roll.

4 Roll out half the mixture at a time, keeping the rest refrigerated. Roll out on a lightly floured surface to about ¼-inch thick. Cut out heart-shaped cookies. Brush away any excess flour on the cookies.

5 Put the cookies on to the prepared baking sheets, spaced apart, and brush with beaten egg white and water to glaze. Sprinkle with sugar.

6 Bake for 15 minutes, until light brown. Remove from the baking sheets and cool on wire racks.

my grandmother's italian cake

torta della mia nonna

I have published this recipe before, but I can't resist including it again, as I have wonderful memories of it being served at special family gatherings, birthdays and feast days. It can be served as an Italian wedding cake, and it is the sort of thing that the local *trattoria* would do for such an occasion, calling it *"torta della casa."* Make it for your family celebrations.

serves 10-12

cake

6 large eggs

1½ cups superfine granulated sugar

1¼ cups all-purpose flour, plus extra for dusting

confectioner's custard

2 tbsp all-purpose flour

2 tbsp superfine granulated sugar

1 large egg

finely grated zest of 1 unwaxed lemon (optional)

½ tsp vanilla extract

1¼ cups milk

butter cream

¾ cup unsalted butter

1½ cups confectioner's sugar,

1 large egg

½ cup cold strong black coffee

topping

1 Preheat the oven to 375ºF. Grease and line a deep 12-inch or 9-inch round cake pan and dust with flour.

2 To make the cake, put the eggs and sugar in a bowl and stand over a saucepan of gently simmering water. Using electric beaters, beat until thick and creamy. Gently sift in the flour a little at a time, and fold in. Pour into the prepared pan. Bake the 12-inch cake for 18-20 minutes, or the 9-inch cake for 35-40 minutes, until risen and golden. Turn out and cool on a wire rack.

3 To make the custard, in a small bowl mix together the flour, sugar, egg, lemon zest (if using) and vanilla extract. Gently heat the milk in a saucepan, but do not allow it to boil. Gradually pour the hot milk into the egg and flour mixture. Return to the saucepan and heat very gently, stirring constantly with a wooden spoon, until the mixture thickens. Remove from the heat and place a piece of parchment paper over the custard to prevent a skin forming. Leave to cool.

method continues on the next page

3 tbsp rum

1¼ cups whipping cream

a few drops of vanilla extract

5 tbsp toasted flaked almonds or
  hazelnuts, or a mixture of both

seasonal fruit or flowers to
  decorate (optional)

4 To make the butter cream, in a bowl beat together the
   butter and the 1½ cups superfine granulated sugar. In a
   separate bowl, beat the egg with the remaining sugar. Add
   the egg and sugar mixture to the butter mixture. Using
   electric beaters, very gently add the coffee (as it can split)
   and mix until thick and creamy.

5 To assemble the cake, cut it horizontally into three even
   layers. Spoon the custard on one layer and spread the
   butter cream on the second. Sandwich the slices together.

6 Gently pour over the rum to soak into the cake. Whip the
   cream and vanilla extract until it just holds its shape,
   then use to cover the top and sides of the cake. Carefully
   press the nuts on to the sides and decorate with fresh
   fruit or flowers if desired. Chill before serving.

stuffed apricots

albicocche ripiene

In the early summer, the orchard at the *Hotel Sante Caleran* provides the chef Eolo with fresh apricots, which he stuffs with amaretti cookies and poaches in amaretti liqueur. Use apricots that are fully ripe yet firm. The best amaretti cookies come in a red box marked *"di Saronna."*

serves 4

10 large firm apricots, about
  1¾lb in total

1¾ tbsp unsalted butter

3 tbsp superfine granulated sugar

⅔ cup amaretti liqueur

12 amaretti cookies, crushed

pine nuts for garnish (optional)

1 Peel the apricots with a vegetable peeler. Cut them in half and remove the pits. Cut two of the halves into large chunks and set aside. Slightly enlarge the hollows in the remaining halves using a melon baller.

2 Melt the butter in a large non-stick frying pan. Add the sugar and cook over medium heat, stirring constantly, until the sugar dissolves and is a light caramel color. Pour in the liqueur. Simmer, stirring, for 2 minutes – it will splutter, so wear oven mitts. Add half the apricots to this syrup and poach for 5-10 minutes, until almost tender (test by piercing with a small sharp knife). Remove with a slotted spoon and drain, inverted, on a shallow plate. Cook the remaining apricots in the same way.

3 Add the crumbled cookies to the syrup left in the pan. Cook over low heat, crushing the crumbs with the back of a wooden spoon until they have melted into a coarse purée. Scrape the contents of the pan into a food processor, add the reserved apricot chunks and process until smooth. Return the mixture to the pan and simmer slowly, stirring constantly, until it is as thick as treacle and dark brown in color. Cool in the pan for 5 minutes. Spoon equal amounts of the filling into the hollows of the apricots. Garnish the top of each apricot with pine nuts, if using.

golden polenta cake
torta di mais

Gabriella runs the *Trattoria di Satornia*, in the Etruscan part of Tuscany bordering on Lazio. Use coarse stone-ground cornmeal, one that you would use to make proper polenta, for this cake. It gives a nutty texture. The cake takes only minutes to assemble – don't even butter and flour the pan. Gabriella lines the pans with parchment paper. Sweet berries are a perfect accompaniment in spring and summer or, when there is a glut of apples, an apple compote. If you like, you can add a handful of raisins or sultanas, soaked in warm water for 10 minutes and drained, to the batter.

serves 6

1¼ cups all-purpose flour

1 cup coarse polenta

1¼ cups superfine granulated sugar

2 tsp baking powder

1 large egg, lightly beaten

¾ cup whole milk

6 tbsp sunflower oil

1 Preheat the oven to 400°F. Line a 9 x 5-inch loaf pan with parchment paper. Allow the paper to extend over the edges of the pan.

2 Combine the flour, polenta, sugar and baking powder in a large mixing bowl and beat thoroughly. Combine the egg, milk and oil and add them to the dry ingredients. Stir with a rubber spatula until the dry ingredients have become moistened. Do not over-work the batter.

3 Pour the batter into the loaf pan, and bake on the center shelf of the oven for 50-55 minutes, or until the cake is golden and a toothpick inserted into the center comes out clean. Transfer to a cooling rack for 10 minutes. Continue to cool it on the rack. Remove the parchment paper just before serving.

desserts & cakes

chocolate and chestnut torte

torta di cioccolato e castagne

This *torte* combines chestnuts – the ultimate organic food – with luxurious chocolate. The recipe comes from Sandra Polo, a baker, who works in the family-run *trattoria* called *Polo*, in the main piazza in Turin. *Polo* is small and friendly, and the food rather rich, decadent even! I like to serve the *torta* with ginger ice-cream and seasonal fruits.

serves 6

½ cup unsalted butter, plus
  extra for greasing
3 tbsp all-purpose flour,
  plus extra for dusting
4 oz bitter couverture
  chocolate or good high
  percentage cocoa butter chocolate
4 large eggs, separated
10½ oz canned, sweetened
  chestnut purée
1 tsp natural vanilla essence
⅛ tsp cream of tartar
½ cup superfine granulated sugar
confectioner's sugar, for dusting

1 Preheat the oven to 350°F. Grease and line a deep 8-inch round cake pan. Dust with flour. Break the chocolate into a bowl and add the butter. Place over a saucepan of simmering water, stirring occasionally, until smooth. Take care not to overheat.

2 Sift the flour into a bowl, add the egg yolks, chestnut purée and vanilla, and whisk. Stir in the chocolate mix.

3 Whisk the egg whites and cream of tartar together until soft peaks form, then gradually whisk in the sugar until stiff. Do not over-beat. Fold a quarter of the egg whites into the chocolate mixture, then carefully fold in the remainder.

4 Pour the mixture into the prepared pan, level with a palette knife, and bake for 40-45 minutes, until a skewer inserted into the center comes out moist but not sticky. Leave to cool in the pan on a rack. It will have risen and then dropped slightly in the center.

5 When cold, turn out and dust with sifted confectioner's sugar.

desserts & cakes

italian chili oil

olio santo

Every *trattoria* in Calabria would have a bottle of this on the table, as would every domestic dining table. It brings a zesty spirit to many dishes such as soup, stews, pasta, rice and salad dressings. Drizzle it on pizza, or dip bread into it if you dare, for it can be "liquid fire!" A bottle of home-made oil makes a wonderful gift.

makes 18 oz

2 tbsp tiny dried chili peppers
  (*peperoncini*)
2⅓ cups good-quality
  olive oil

1 Put the chili peppers in a small glass jar. If you want a garlic and herb-scented *olio santo*, add 4 peeled garlic cloves and 1 tsp dried oregano to the jar.

2 Pour the olive oil over the chili peppers, seal the lid tightly and store in a cool dark place for a week, shaking occasionally.

3 Once the oil has steeped for a week, strain and throw away the chili peppers (and other flavorings, if used). Wash and thoroughly dry the jar, then pour the oil back into it and re-seal.

green tomato preserve

marmellata di pomodori verdi

A sweet, tart, green tomato preserve complements a young pecorino as well as one that is more mature. It is also good with most other cheeses and with toasted bread for breakfast. Green tomatoes begin to appear in mid or late spring. Select firm, unripe tomatoes and use them quickly. This is one of my grandmother's recipes, and I very clearly remember the mass of green tomatoes on her terrace at certain times of the year.

makes about 3lb

1 unwaxed lemon

4lb unripe, green tomatoes, cored, halved and sliced ½-inch thick

7½ cups superfine granulated sugar

4 tbsp runny honey

1 Rinse six 8-oz jam jars with screw-top lids in warm soapy water. Place a rack at the bottom of a large pot. Open the jars and rest them on the rack with the lids. Fill the pot with boiling water to cover the jars by 1 inch and boil for 10 minutes. Remove the jars and lids with tongs. Invert them on to a cooling rack and cool and dry completely.

2 Peel the zest off the lemon in long sections and cut into julienne strips. Cut the lemon lengthwise in half, remove the seeds and slice into ¼-inch thick slices. Combine the green tomato slices, lemon slices, lemon zest, sugar, honey and 1 cup water in a large heavy pot. Bring to a boil and simmer gently for 1½-1¾ hours, stirring often, or until the preserve has thickened. Reduce the heat if the mixture begins to stick. To test if reduced enough, place a spoonful of preserve on a small saucer and freeze for 5 minutes. When cold, the preserve should be thick like marmalade. Continue cooking and testing as necessary.

3 When ready, spoon the preserve into the sterilized jars, leaving ½-inch headspace. Use a clean damp cloth to wipe away drips. Cool the jars completely. When cool, seal the jars with the lids. Store in the fridge for up to two months.

home-made ricotta cheese
ricotta fatta in casa

If ricotta cheese is unavailable, try making this version in your own
kitchen. It's doubly useful to me now that I live in the country, and can't
just pop out to the local deli. It's ideal for making *pizza rustica*, a savory
ricotta pie as served in the *Trattoria Paola Bina* in Naples – a filling of
ricotta, mozzarella, salami and eggs, all encased in pastry.

makes 8 oz

4¼ cups fresh whole milk

1 tsp salt

4 tsp lemon juice

1 Place the milk, salt and lemon juice in a saucepan. Bring
to a boil, then simmer for 15 minutes, or until the curds
float on the top.

2 Transfer the curds to a square of muslin using a
slotted spoon, tie up and hang over the sink to drain for
2-3 hours. Your cheese is ready!

bocconcini marinated with herbs
bocconcini con erbe in marinata

Serve *bocconcini* – miniature mozzarella cheeses – sliced with assorted salad leaves and a little of the marinade spooned over. This makes a delicious *antipasto*, especially at dinner parties. A jar also makes a wonderful gift.

fills 2 x 8-oz jars

18 oz fresh *bocconcini*,
  drained and dried

3 garlic cloves, peeled

2 sprigs each oregano and thyme

a handful of fresh flat-leaf parsley

3 fresh bay leaves

3 small red chilies

¾ cup fruity extra virgin
  olive oil

1 Place the *bocconcini*, garlic, oregano, thyme, parsley, bay
   leaves and chilies in clean, sterilized jars (see page 242).

2 Cover the *bocconcini* and other ingredients with olive
   oil. Seal the jars and refrigerate, it will keep for up to
   two weeks.

chickpeas in garlic oil

ceci in olio e aglio

I have a great love for pulses, and Campania, my home region, is famous for its chickpeas. They are served as an *antipasto* misto in many of the *trattorias*, and are also on sale in jars. Cannellini and borlotti beans can be treated in the same way. Serve at room temperature.

fills 1 x 18fl oz jar

¾ cup dried chickpeas

1¼ cups extra virgin olive oil

4 garlic cloves, peeled and crushed

freshly ground black pepper

3 tbsp lemon juice

a handful of fresh flat-leaf parsley, chopped

1 Place the chickpeas in a small saucepan, cover with cold water, bring to a boil and turn off the heat. Cover and soak for 1 hour. Drain and cover with fresh cold water. Cover the pan, boil for 10 minutes, then cook over low heat for 2-3 hours or until tender. Drain well.

2 Heat the oil in a frying pan and cook the garlic and chickpeas until lightly browned. Season to taste with black pepper and mix in the lemon juice and parsley.

3 Pack the chickpeas and oil into a warm sterilized jar (see page 242), and leave to go cold before refrigerating until required. Allow to infuse for up to four days. You can keep them for up to a month in the refrigerator.

home-made mascarpone cheese
mascarpone fatto in casa

If mascarpone is unavailable, this recipe makes a wonderful alternative.
You will find that the curd will turn more quickly in warmer weather.

makes 8 oz

1½ cups extra thick whipping
cream

3 tbsp buttermilk

1 Place the cream in a saucepan and heat to lukewarm,
90°F. Pour into a bowl and stir in the buttermilk, cover
and set aside to stand for 24-48 hours or until a soft
curd forms.

2 Dip a piece of muslin large enough to line a colander in
cold water, then wring dry. Line the colander
with muslin and place in the sink. Pour the
curd into the colander and set aside to drain
for about 10 minutes.

3 Fold the muslin over the curd and place the
colander on a rack in a baking dish. Cover the
colander and baking dish with plastic wrap.
Refrigerate for 36-48 hours.

4 To serve, spoon the cheese into a dish and
use. Keep in the refrigerator for up to four to
five days.

bolognese pickled onions
cipolle sottaceto alla bolognese

This recipe comes from a chef in central Bologna, the gastronomic capital of Italy. The onions are so popular that Signor Bartolini also sells them (and I think a jar is great as a gift).

fills a 9 oz jar

2 tbsp sea salt

1 tsp superfine granulated sugar

15 small white onions, peeled

3 fresh bay leaves

2½ cups red wine vinegar (a good-quality one will make a big difference)

1 Place 4¼ cups water, the salt and sugar in a saucepan and bring to a boil. Add the onions and cook for 2 minutes. Drain the onions and pat them dry with absorbent paper towel. Set aside to cool completely.

2 Place the onions and bay leaves in a warm, sterilized jar (see page 244). Cover with vinegar and seal. Store in a dark place for a month.

green sauce with capers and herbs
salsa verde

This can be served as a dip for an appetizer with crusty bread or *crudités*, or on *crostini*. It's a classical sauce, showing the Italian love of things vinegary – the gherkins, capers and vinegar (all of which are appetite stimulants). It will keep in the fridge for about four days.

serves 4

4 pickled cucumbers or big gherkins

1 large bunch fresh flat-leaf parsley

1 oz fresh mint leaves

1 oz salted capers, rinsed and dried

2 garlic cloves, peeled and chopped

2 large eggs, hard-boiled

4 tbsp fresh breadcrumbs

2 tbsp white wine vinegar

1 tbsp superfine granulated sugar

8 tbsp extra virgin olive oil

sea salt and freshly ground black pepper

1 Finely chop the cucumbers, parsley, mint, capers and garlic. Mash the hard-boiled eggs.

2 Put all the ingredients in a food processor and blend everything together to produce a smooth, green sauce. Serve cold.

vegetable broth
brodo di verdure

This is a light but flavorful broth that is good for vegetable-based soups and sauces.

makes about 6⅓ cups

1 tbsp olive oil

2¾ tbsp unsalted butter

3 garlic cloves, peeled and crushed

1 large onion, peeled and chopped

4 leeks, trimmed and chopped

2 carrots, scrubbed and chopped

2 celery stalks, chopped

1 fennel bulb, halved

a handful of fresh flat-leaf parsley

4 bay leaves

2 sprigs fresh thyme

1 Heat the oil and butter together in a large saucepan or stockpot, then fry the garlic gently for 2 minutes.

2 Add all the remaining vegetables and herbs and cook over low heat, stirring constantly, until softened but not browned.

3 Add 12⅔ cups water and bring to a boil. Reduce the heat, cover and leave to simmer for an hour.

4 Strain the stock and return to the pan, discarding the solids. Boil rapidly until reduced by half. Allow to cool, then refrigerate and use within three days, or freeze.

chicken broth

brodo di pollo

The best chicken broths are made with a fresh raw chicken, but a good substitute can be made with a cooked carcass.

makes 6⅓ cups

1 x 3lb chicken

2 medium onions, peeled and quartered

2 celery stalks

1 large potato, peeled and quartered

3 bay leaves

a handful of fresh flat-leaf parsley

1 Wash the chicken in cold water and cut off any visible fat. Bring water to a boil in a large saucepan or stockpot.

2 Add the chicken to the hot water along with all the remaining ingredients. Bring back to a boil and boil rapidly for 5 minutes.

3 Reduce the heat to low, then simmer very slowly, uncovered, for about 2 hours. Top up with more water if necessary to keep the chicken covered. Skim off any scum from time to time.

4 Remove the chicken from the broth, then strain the broth through a fine sieve. Discard the chicken and allow the broth to cool.

5 Chill the broth, then remove the layer of fat that will form on the surface. Keep refrigerated for up to five days, or freeze.

cheeses, preserves, oils & broths

beef broth
brodo di carne

A meat broth can be made with any meat, not just beef, but those made from lamb or pork will taste very much stronger. The recipe here is a simplified version of the most elaborate and tasty of beef broths, which can involve veal bones as well as beef, chicken wings and a pig's foot to give the finished broth extra flavor and a gelatinous quality.

makes 6⅓ cups

2¼lb raw beef bones and
    scraps, or about that weight of
    beef shin
2 large onions, peeled and
    quartered
3 celery stalks, halved
1 head garlic, halved
2 carrots, scrubbed
2 large plum tomatoes
3 bay leaves

1 Preheat the oven to 400°F/.

2 Put the beef bones and pieces, or the shin, into a roasting pan with the onion, and roast for about 30 minutes, turning every now and again. Drain off any oil.

3 Put all the ingredients (including the roasted meat and onion) into a large saucepan or stockpot. Cover with water and bring to a boil for about 5 minutes.

4 Reduce the heat to low, and then simmer very slowly, half covered, for about 2-3 hours. Top up with more water if necessary to keep the chicken covered. Skim off any scum from time to time. Do not let the liquid do more than bubble gently.

5 Remove the bones and meat from the broth, then strain the broth through a fine sieve. Discard the bones and meat and allow the broth to cool.

6 Chill the broth, then remove the layer of fat that will form on the surface. Keep refrigerated for up to five days, or freeze.

Index

Index